Cooking at a Glance

Cookies

Published by Fog City Press
814 Montgomery Street
San Francisco, CA 94133 USA

Chief Executive Officer John Owen

President Terry Newell

Art Director Kylie Mulquin

Editorial Manager Janine Flew

Production Manager Gilly Biven

Production Coordinator Kylie Lawson

Business Manager Emily Jahn

Vice President International Sales
Stuart Laurence

Project Managing Editor Tori Ritchie

Contributing Editor Jane Horn

Project Designer Patty Hill

Food Photographer Chris Shorten

Steps Photographer Kevin Candland

Food Stylists Susan Massey
and Vicki Roberts-Russell

Prop Stylist Laura Ferguson

A catalog record for this book is
available from the Library of Congress,
Washington, DC.

ISBN 1-892374-47-1

Manufactured by Kyodo Printing Co.
(S'pore) Pte Ltd
Printed in Singapore
A Weldon Owen Production

Cover Recipe: Assorted Cookies,
pages 25, 46, 56, 70, 82, and 108
Opposite Page: Triple-Chocolate Cookies,
page 24

CONTENTS

INTRODUCTION 6

THE BASICS 7

Storing Cookies 12

DROP COOKIES 13

BAR COOKIES 31

CUTOUT COOKIES 49

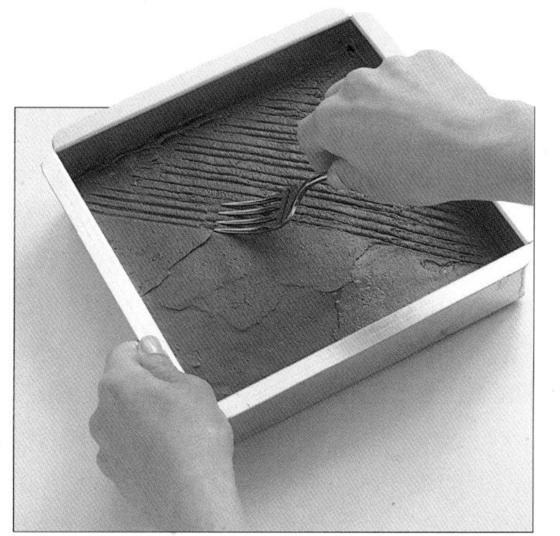

Sliced Cookies 67

Shaped & Molded Cookies 79

Pressed Cookies 95

Specialty Cookies 107

Glossary 118

Index 120

Introduction

IT IS HARD — no, it's almost impossible — to keep a cookie jar filled. No matter how many batches of vanilla-scented sugar cookies, craggy, chocolate-dotted drop cookies, or elegant meringue kisses come out of the oven, they seem to disappear almost before they cool. And it isn't only little hands that reach for these delectable treats. Everyone succumbs to their allure.

In this collection of recipes from Better Homes and Gardens®, you will find many that will evoke sweet memories of childhood favorites lovingly prepared in a kitchen perfumed with the warm smells of spices. Others will be entirely new, created to appeal to more sophisticated, grown-up tastes. All reflect our one hundred-plus years of combined test-kitchen experience that ensures a successful result every time you bake.

Like each volume in the *Cooking at a Glance* series, the recipes are presented in a vivid step-by-step format designed for cooks of all skill levels. Every important stage of cookie making, from measuring to mixing to shaping, plus all the professional tricks for decorating and finishing, is included. Each is explained in easy-to-understand language and presented in full-color photographs. It's all there at a glance, as if you were back in your grandmother's kitchen or looking over the shoulder of one of our test-kitchen professionals.

An introductory chapter covers the basics, including how to properly store finished cookies to maintain their just-baked freshness. Succeeding chapters highlight a particular type of cookie, including all the favorites: drop cookies, bars, whimsical cutouts, sliced, shaped, and molded cookies, pressed spritz, and specialties such as French madeleines and Italian biscotti. Every chapter is color-coded and each recipe features a "steps-at-a-glance" box that uses these colors for quick reference to the photographic steps necessary for its preparation. Tips appear on virtually every page, from basic equipment needs to helpful hints to a glossary of ingredients.

Throughout these pages you will be delighted with the variety of ideas, including a charming gingerbread cottage just the right size for cookie "architects" of all ages to work on during the holidays. Consider this book your personal recipe file. Don't hesitate to make notes, if you need to, when variations come to mind. The recipes are so inventive and the directions so clearly explained that you just might create something entirely new as you go along. It's all there, *at a glance*.

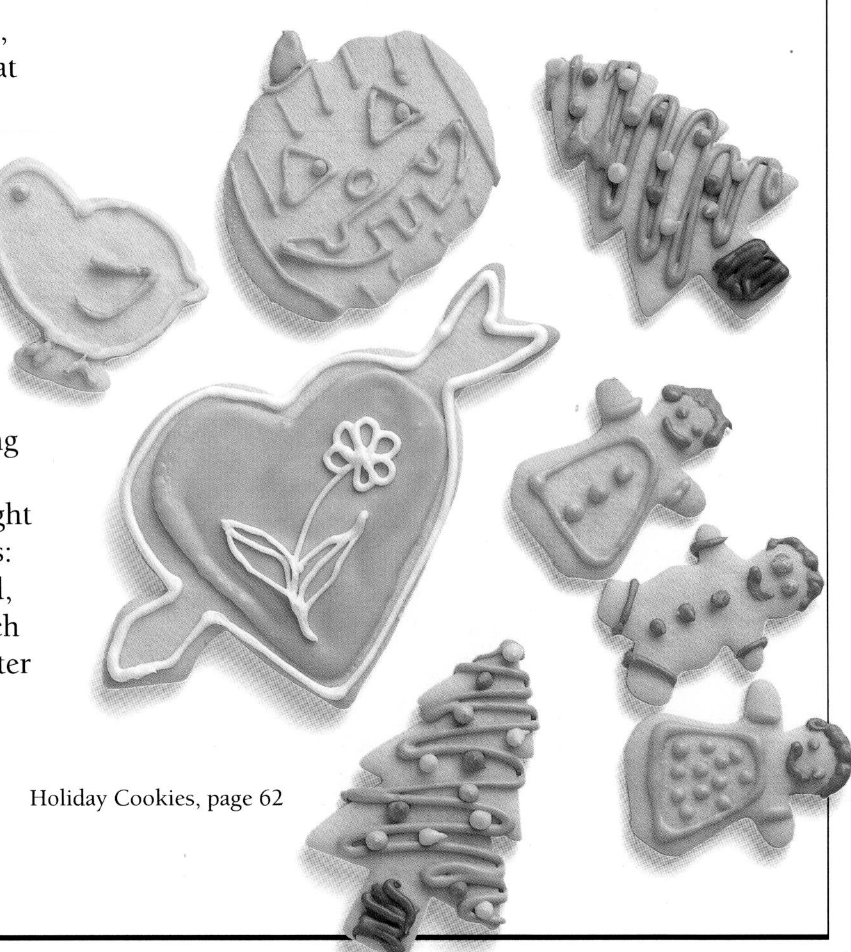

Holiday Cookies, page 62

The Basics

Steps for Making Cookie Dough

Basic Tools for Making Cookie Dough

If you bake, you probably have the equipment you'll need for making cookie dough: an electric mixer and bowl, measuring cups, spatulas, knives, a cutting board, and spoons.

No other kind of baking is as simple and informal as making cookies. Whether you are a long-time cookie baker or a novice enthusiast, you will find inspiration in the pages that follow. The basic techniques demonstrated in this chapter will give you the skills to keep your cookie jar filled with the irresistible confections that appear in every chapter of this book.

Success also depends on using the right equipment. For best results, bake on cookie sheets made from shiny, heavyweight aluminum with low sides or with a lip on one edge. Baking pans with high, straight sides will block heat and cause cookies to bake unevenly, while insulated sheets heat so slowly that cookies may require a different baking time than specified in these recipes. Also avoid dark sheets, as they absorb heat and may cause overbrowning. While the best procedure is to bake on the center rack of your oven, you can stagger two sheets at one time and switch positions halfway through baking to allow even exposure to heat.

unless the recipe calls for it, there is no need to sift all-purpose flour

STEP 1 Measuring Flour

Before spooning the flour into the measuring cup, stir it lightly with a fork in the canister to lighten it. Then fill the cup with flour, but don't pack it down. Level by sweeping across the top with a small metal spatula or a knife.

when measuring granulated sugar, spoon it into a dry measuring cup, then level off with a spatula

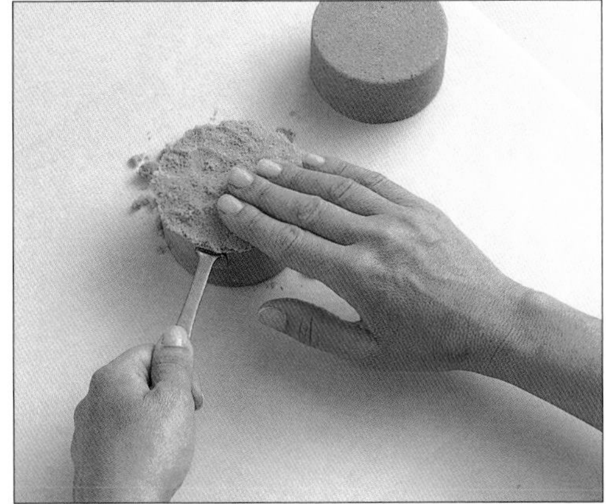

STEP 2 **Measuring Brown Sugar**

Spoon brown sugar into the measuring cup so that it rises in a mound slightly above the rim. Press the brown sugar firmly into the cup with your hand. To unmold, turn upside down; the sugar will hold the shape of the cup.

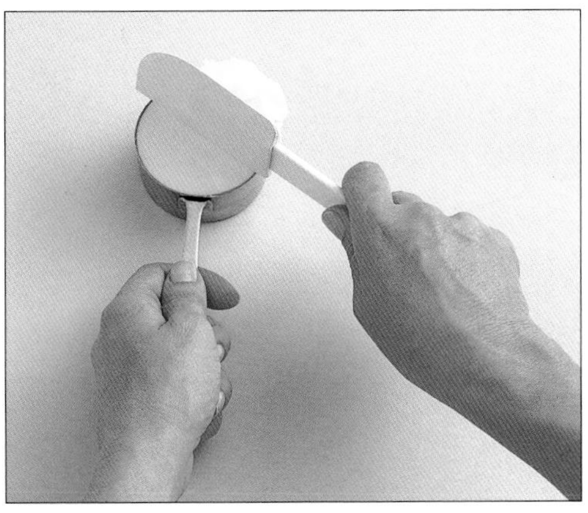

STEP 3 **Measuring Shortening**

Fill a measuring cup with shortening. Press the shortening firmly into the cup with a rubber spatula. Level off by sweeping across the rim with the spatula or a knife.

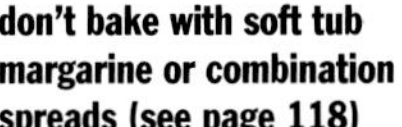

don't bake with soft tub margarine or combination spreads (see page 118)

STEP 4 **Measuring Butter (Margarine)**

Don't have the butter or margarine too soft or it won't cut cleanly and accurately. With a sharp knife, cut through the butter or margarine following the measurement guidelines printed on the paper. Let soften fully before making dough.

sticky liquids like honey will pour out smoothly if the measuring cup is first brushed lightly with oil

set the cup flat on the counter so the surface of the liquid aligns with the markings

STEP 5 **Measuring Liquids**

Set a glass or plastic liquid measuring cup on a counter or tabletop. Add the liquid. For greatest accuracy, check the measurement at eye level rather than from above.

scrape the sides of the bowl once or twice with a rubber spatula

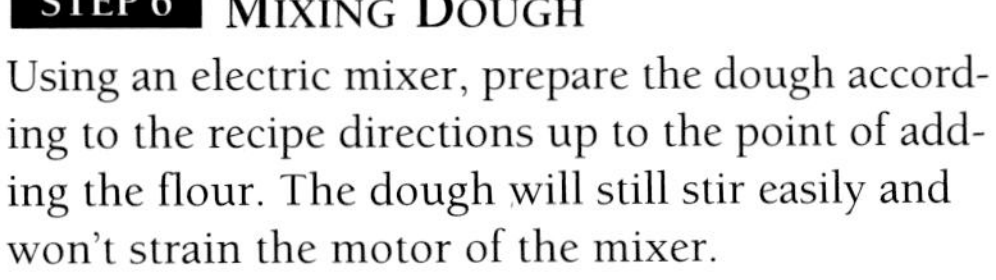

STEP 6 **Mixing Dough**

Using an electric mixer, prepare the dough according to the recipe directions up to the point of adding the flour. The dough will still stir easily and won't strain the motor of the mixer.

some portable mixers do not have motors that are powerful enough to incorporate all of the flour

STEP 7 **Stirring in Remaining Flour**

Beat in as much flour as you can using the electric mixer (the dough will become stiff). Stir in any remaining flour by hand with a wooden spoon until the dough is a homogeneous mixture with no streaks of flour showing.

Steps for Making Toppings and Meringue

Basic Tools for Making Toppings and Meringue

Essential equipment for preparing toppings and meringue includes an electric mixer and mixing bowls, spoons for measuring and stirring, a baking pan, wire rack, and fine-meshed sieve, and a small saucepan for melting chocolate.

MIXING BOWL

ELECTRIC MIXER

BAKING PAN AND WIRE RACK

FINE-MESHED SIEVE AND PAPER TOWEL

WOODEN SPOON

SMALL SAUCEPAN

SPOON

MEASURING SPOON

SMALL BOWL

Chocolate, sugar, eggs, nuts: These ingredients turn up again and again in every type of cookie, whether dropped from a spoon, baked in a pan, piped from a pastry bag, or formed with a cutter. The steps on these pages explain how to achieve a few of the more common uses for these popular additions. Not only will you come across these techniques in recipes throughout the book, you'll also find them basic to almost all types of baking, so they are good tricks to know. You will learn how to melt chocolate to flavor dough or to decorate it, to make that miraculous cloud-like product of egg white and sugar called meringue, to toast nuts so they are aromatic and rich, and to apply icing in a network of fine lines, a technique known as drizzling (another way to create this effective finishing touch is to pipe from a plastic bag as shown on page 17).

the chocolate will melt more quickly if first broken into small pieces

stirring over low heat prevents the chocolate on the bottom of the pan from scorching

STEP 1 Melting Chocolate

Place chocolate pieces and shortening (if called for) in a small, heavy saucepan. Cook over low heat, stirring often, until melted and smooth. Or, place in a glass dish and microwave on high power for 1 to 3 minutes, or melt in a heavy-duty plastic bag as shown on page 17.

toasting nuts enhances their flavor and deepens their color

STEP 2 Toasting Nuts

Preheat an oven to 350°. Spread the nut halves or pieces in a single layer in a shallow baking pan. Bake until the nuts have colored slightly to a light, golden brown, about 5 to 10 minutes. Stir once or twice with a wooden spoon so the nuts brown evenly.

nuts used for topping look better without this papery skin; this step isn't necessary for nuts stirred into a batter

STEP 3 Sifting Nuts

After the nuts have been toasted and chopped (if called for), spoon them into a fine wire-mesh sieve set over paper toweling. Tap the edge of the sifter to filter out the skin of the nuts.

Lacy lines of icing dress up cutout cookies like Molasses & Ginger Stars (page 64).

you can also drizzle icing or chocolate with a fork or, for a more regular pattern, with a pastry bag and small round tip, or with a plastic bag (see page 17)

STEP 4 Drizzling Icing or Chocolate

Arrange cooled cookies on a wire rack over waxed paper. Fill a small spoon with icing or melted chocolate. Move the spoon back and forth over each cookie to create fine lines. Let the icing or chocolate flow off the spoon in a ribbon.

TIP BOX

Making Meringue

STEP 1 Adding Sugar

With an electric mixer on medium speed, beat the egg whites until they are white and foamy and the tips of the peaks bend over when the beaters are lifted out (soft peaks). Gradually add sugar, 1 tablespoon at a time.

STEP 2 Beating to Stiff Peaks

Continue beating the egg whites and sugar until the mixture begins to stiffen. The meringue is ready when it looks glossy and forms stiff peaks when the beaters are lifted out.

Steps for Storing Cookies

Basic Tools for Storing Cookies

To keep cookies fresh, store them in airtight containers between layers of waxed paper.

COOKIE JAR

PLASTIC CONTAINERS

COOKIE TIN

WAXED PAPER

ALTHOUGH IT IS a rare batch that lasts more than a few days without being devoured down to the very last crumb, cookies can stale quickly unless protected against air or excess moisture. Proper storage also prevents them from breakage or other damage.

Let cookies cool completely, then arrange in an airtight container as shown in the step at right. They will keep at room temperature for up to 3 days. If you prefer, leave bar cookies in their baking pan, tightly covered with plastic wrap or aluminum foil. Store soft and crisp cookies separately, or the crisp ones will absorb moisture from the others and become soft themselves. On the other hand, you can revive soft cookies that have dried out and hardened by placing a wedge of apple or a slice of bread on a piece of waxed paper and setting it on top of the cookies in the closed container. Remove after 1 day.

For longer storage, freeze unfrosted cookies in heavy-duty freezer bags or freezer containers. They will stay fresh up to 1 year. When needed, thaw and decorate.

STEP 1 Storing Cookies

Select a storage container that allows easy access to the cookies inside. Arrange the cookies in layers in the container. If the cookies are soft, place a sheet of waxed paper between each layer. Seal the container airtight.

Drop Cookies

Steps for Making Drop Cookies

Basic Tools for Making Drop Cookies

Use a large bowl and wooden spoon for drop cookie dough, plus smaller bowls for additions like nuts or dried fruit. A pair of tablespoons or teaspoons is all you need to transfer the dough to the cookie sheet. Transfer cookies to a cooling rack with a wide metal spatula.

COOLING RACK

LARGE AND SMALL BOWLS

COOKIE SHEET

SPOONS

WOODEN SPOON

METAL SPATULA

MAKING DROP COOKIES is a simple craft. No artistry is required, only a gentle push to transfer the dough from spoon to cookie sheet. As they bake, the soft, chunky mounds spread and settle into charmingly irregular rounds with a homey appeal that are perfect with a good cup of coffee or a frosty glass of milk.

Not only are drop cookies easy to prepare, but they have a wonderful versatility. By varying a few ingredients or adjusting the proportions, you can change this kind of cookie dramatically. Their texture can be chewy, like the cookies used to make Ice Cream Sandwiches (page 22), or soft and tender, like fruit-filled Orange-Fig Drops (page 26). They needn't even use a traditional dough: Amaretti (page 18), for example, are made from a frothy mixture of egg whites, sugar, and ground almonds.

STEP 1 Stirring in Ingredients

After mixing the basic dough (see pages 8 and 9), beat in as much of the flour as you can with the mixer. Then, mix in remaining flour and other ingredients with a wooden spoon.

for uniform results, you could use a small, spring-loaded ice cream scoop to shape and drop cookies

STEP 2 Dropping Dough

Scoop up the dough with a small metal spoon. With the back of another spoon or a rubber spatula, push the dough onto a cookie sheet.

a chocolate cookie is done if the imprint of your fingertip on its top is barely visible

STEP 3 Testing for Doneness

When done, the cookies will be lightly browned on the bottom. Check by lifting one cookie with a spatula to see the color of its underside. The dough should also feel set.

cookies that are too soft to move should remain on the cookie sheet for an extra minute or two to firm up

STEP 4 Cooling on a Rack

After the cookies have finished baking, remove them from the cookie sheet with a metal spatula that is big enough to support the whole cookie, and transfer to a wire rack to cool completely.

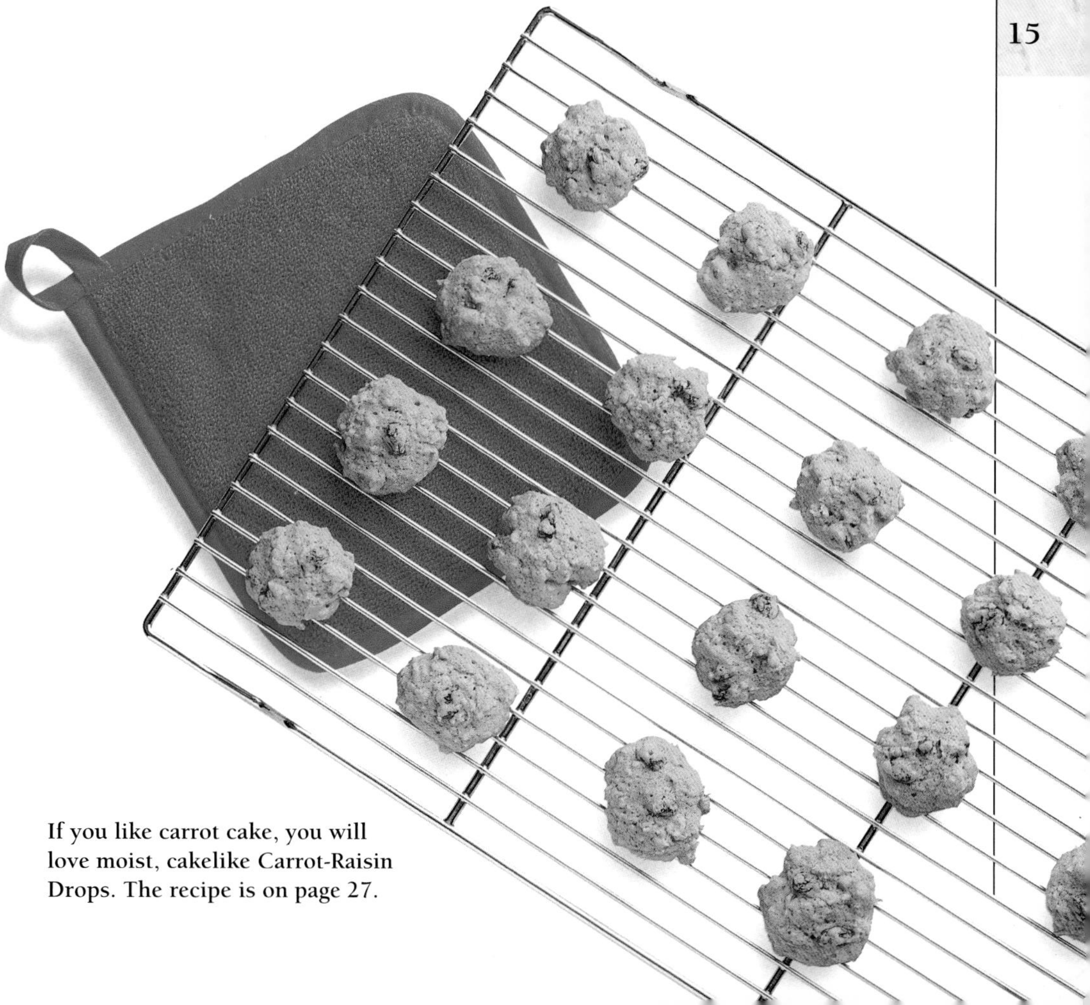

If you like carrot cake, you will love moist, cakelike Carrot-Raisin Drops. The recipe is on page 27.

A delicious after-dinner sweet, these sophisticated drop cookies blend rich chocolate with aromatic toasted nuts.

Chocolate-drizzled Praline Cookies

INGREDIENTS

1/2	CUP BUTTER *OR* MARGARINE, SOFTENED
1	CUP PACKED BROWN SUGAR
1-1/2	TEASPOONS BAKING POWDER
1	EGG
2	TEASPOONS VANILLA
1-1/2	CUPS ALL-PURPOSE FLOUR
1	CUP TOASTED CHOPPED PECANS *OR* WALNUTS
1/2	CUP SEMISWEET CHOCOLATE PIECES
1	TEASPOON SHORTENING

Be careful not to overbake these pecan-loaded treats: they are best when nice and chewy. Begin to check for doneness after about 5 minutes.

■ In a mixing bowl beat the butter or margarine with an electric mixer on medium to high speed for 30 seconds. Add the brown sugar and baking powder; beat till combined. Beat in the egg and vanilla. Beat in as much of the flour as you can with the mixer. Stir in any remaining flour with a wooden spoon. Stir in the pecans or walnuts.

■ Drop dough by rounded teaspoons 2 inches apart onto ungreased cookie sheets. Bake in a preheated 375° oven for 8 to 10 minutes, or till bottoms are golden brown. Remove cookies and cool on wire racks.

■ In a small, heavy-duty plastic bag, combine chocolate pieces and shortening. Close bag just above chocolate, then set sealed bag in a bowl of warm water till melted. With scissors, snip off ⅛ inch of the corner of the bag. Gently squeeze the bag to pipe chocolate mixture over cookies. Or, melt chocolate and shortening in a saucepan over low heat. Let cool 5 minutes, then drizzle over cookies with a spoon. Let stand till chocolate is set.

Makes about 32 cookies

Per cookie: 107 calories, 2 g protein, 13 g carbohydrate, 6 g total fat (2 g saturated), 14 mg cholesterol, 38 mg sodium, 63 mg potassium

Preparation Time: 20 minutes
Baking Time: 8 to 10 minutes

STEPS AT A GLANCE	Page
MAKING COOKIE DOUGH	8
TOASTING NUTS	11
MAKING DROP COOKIES	14
PIPING CHOCOLATE	17

STEPS FOR PIPING CHOCOLATE

STEP 1 MELTING CHOCOLATE IN BAG
Place both chocolate and shortening in a heavy-duty plastic bag and push all to one corner. Tie the bag just above this mixture, then set the bag in a bowl of warm water to melt. Rub to blend the contents.

STEP 2 SNIPPING BAG
Invert the bag so the tip faces upward. Squeeze a little of the melted mixture away from the tip, then snip off a tiny piece from the corner to create an opening.

STEP 3 PIPING CHOCOLATE
Squeeze the bag gently to pipe out the chocolate in a steady stream. Move back and forth across the cookies, set on a wire rack, to create a network of lines.

Amaretti

STEPS AT A GLANCE

STEPS AT A GLANCE	Page
MAKING MERINGUE	11
MAKING DROP COOKIES	14
PREPARING PANS & GRINDING NUTS	18

Preparation Time: 45 minutes
Baking Time: 12 to 15 minutes
Cooling Time: 30 minutes

INGREDIENTS

2	EGG WHITES
1-1/4	CUPS BLANCHED WHOLE ALMONDS
3/4	CUP GRANULATED SUGAR
1/4	TEASPOON CREAM OF TARTAR
1/4	TEASPOON ALMOND EXTRACT
1/4	CUP SLIVERED ALMONDS

Perfect for a light ending to a big meal, amaretti are puffy confections served frequently in Italy. A cup of espresso or cappuccino would be the perfect complement.

■ In a large mixing bowl let the egg whites stand at room temperature for 30 minutes. Meanwhile, line 2 cookie sheets with parchment paper or brown kraft paper. Set aside. In a food processor bowl or blender container process or blend whole almonds with ¼ cup of the sugar till almonds are finely ground. Set aside.

■ Add the cream of tartar and almond extract to the egg whites. Beat with an electric mixer on medium speed till soft peaks form (tips curl). Gradually add the remaining ½ cup sugar, 1 tablespoon at a time, beating on high speed till very stiff peaks form (tips stand straight) and sugar is almost dissolved. Fold in ground almonds.

■ Drop meringue mixture by rounded teaspoons 1½ inches apart onto the prepared cookie sheets. Sprinkle a few slivered almonds over each cookie. Bake in a preheated 300° oven for 12 to 15 minutes, or till cookies just begin to brown (centers will be soft). Turn off oven. Let cookies dry in oven with the door closed for 30 minutes. Peel cookies from paper. Store in an airtight container in a cool, dry place for up to 1 week.

Makes about 40 cookies

Per cookie: 43 calories, 1 g protein, 5 g carbohydrate, 2 g total fat (0 g saturated), 0 mg cholesterol, 3 mg sodium, 38 mg potassium

STEPS FOR PREPARING PANS AND GRINDING NUTS

STEP 1 LINING COOKIE SHEET
Cut a sheet of parchment paper to fit the cookie sheet. If your supermarket or kitchenware store doesn't carry parchment paper, substitute brown kraft paper.

STEP 2 GRINDING NUTS
Put the almonds and ¼ cup of the sugar in a food processor or blender. Process or blend until the nuts are finely ground, but still light and dry. Don't overgrind, or the nuts will turn to paste.

The nutty sweetness of almonds permeates a classic Italian meringue drop that is baked until barely browned, then slowly cooled until dry and crisp.

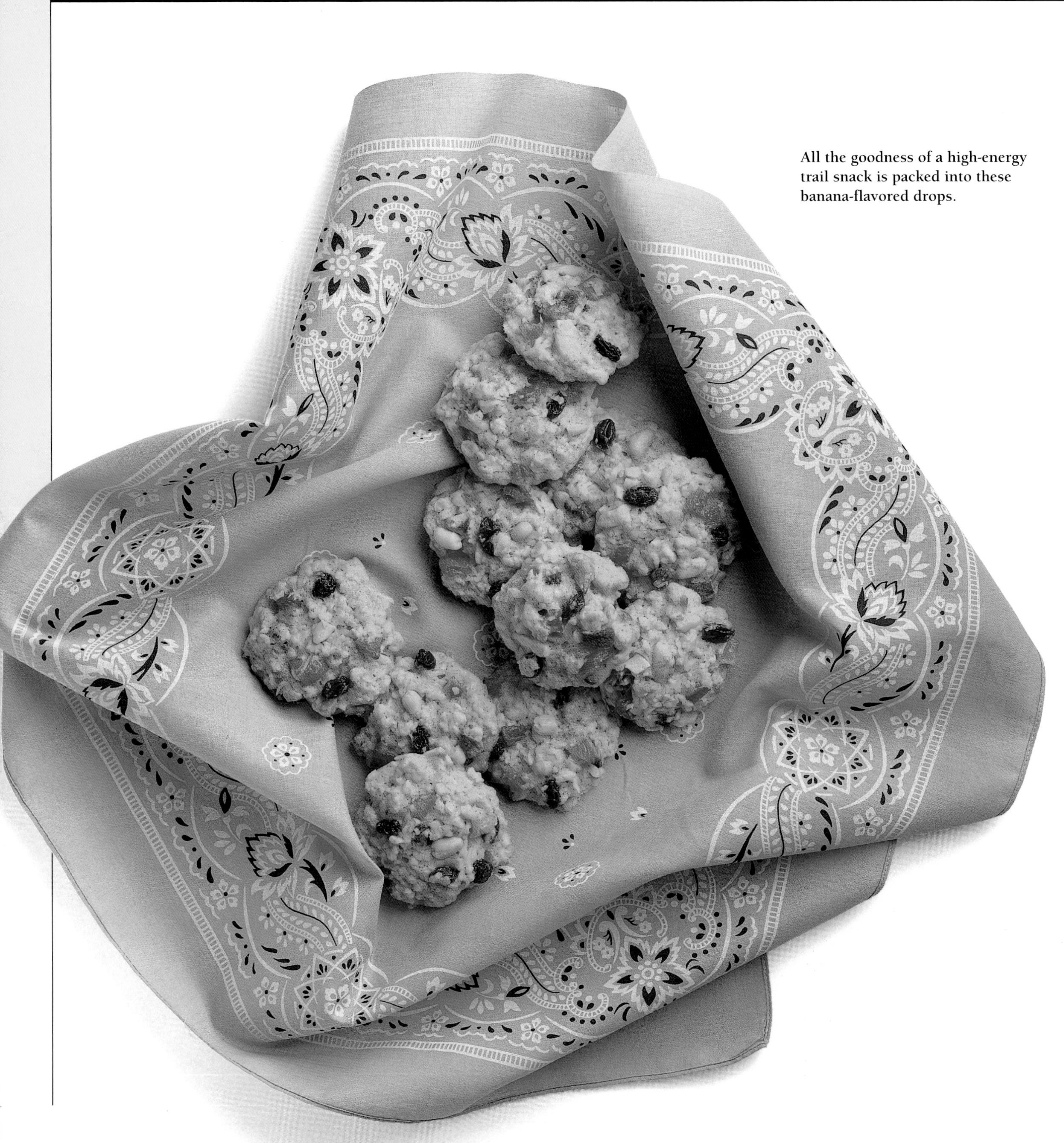

All the goodness of a high-energy trail snack is packed into these banana-flavored drops.

Trail Mix Cookies

STEPS AT A GLANCE	Page
PREPARING FRUIT	21
MAKING COOKIE DOUGH	8
MAKING DROP COOKIES	14

If desired, substitute 2½ cups of prepared trail mix containing fruit, nuts, and coconut for the dried fruits, coconut, and chopped nuts called for in this recipe. Be sure to break up any banana chips and whole nuts, and snip any other large pieces of dried fruit into bits.

■ In a large mixing bowl beat the butter or margarine with an electric mixer on medium to high speed for 30 seconds. Add the granulated sugar, brown sugar, baking powder, baking soda, and allspice; beat till combined. Beat in the eggs, mashed bananas, and vanilla. Beat in as much of the flour as you can with the mixer. Stir in any remaining flour with a wooden spoon. Stir in the oats, dried fruit bits, coconut, and nuts.

■ Drop dough by rounded tablespoons 2 inches apart onto ungreased cookie sheets. Bake in a preheated 375° oven for 10 to 12 minutes, or till golden brown. Remove cookies and cool on wire racks.

Makes about 48 cookies

Per cookie: 98 calories, 2 g protein, 13 g carbohydrate, 5 g total fat (2 g saturated), 16 mg cholesterol, 62 mg sodium, 85 mg potassium

Preparation Time: 20 minutes
Baking Time: 10 to 12 minutes

INGREDIENTS

3/4	CUP BUTTER *OR* MARGARINE, SOFTENED
1/2	CUP GRANULATED SUGAR
1/2	CUP PACKED BROWN SUGAR
1	TEASPOON BAKING POWDER
1/2	TEASPOON BAKING SODA
1	TEASPOON GROUND ALLSPICE
2	EGGS
1	CUP MASHED BANANAS (3 MEDIUM)
1	TEASPOON VANILLA
1-1/2	CUPS ALL-PURPOSE FLOUR
1-1/2	CUPS ROLLED OATS
1	CUP MIXED DRIED FRUIT BITS
3/4	CUP COCONUT
3/4	CUP CHOPPED PEANUTS, WALNUTS, *OR* PECANS

STEPS FOR PREPARING FRUIT

STEP 1 MASHING BANANAS

Break up the peeled bananas into several pieces. Place the pieces in a pie plate or shallow bowl and crush with a fork or a vegetable masher.

STEP 2 SNIPPING FRUIT

If using trail mix instead of chopped dried fruit, snip any large pieces of fruit into bits with kitchen scissors. If the blades get sticky, wipe them clean, then spray with a nonstick vegetable spray.

Ice Cream Sandwiches

INGREDIENTS

1	CUP BUTTER *OR* MARGARINE, SOFTENED
2/3	CUP GRANULATED SUGAR
2	TEASPOONS BAKING POWDER
1/4	TEASPOON SALT
2	EGGS
1/3	CUP HONEY
1-1/2	CUPS ALL-PURPOSE FLOUR
3/4	CUP ROLLED OATS
1/2	CUP SEMISWEET CHOCOLATE PIECES *AND/OR* RAISINS *AND/OR* SNIPPED DRIED FRUIT
1	QUART VANILLA, CHOCOLATE, RUM RAISIN, CHOCOLATE CHIP *OR* YOUR CHOICE OF ICE CREAM

The ice cream will be a lot easier to work with if you let it soften slightly before packing it into the measuring cup. Let your imagination have free rein when choosing your ice cream flavor.

■ In a mixing bowl beat the butter or margarine with an electric mixer on medium to high speed for 30 seconds. Add the sugar, baking powder, and salt; beat till combined. Beat in the eggs and honey. Beat in as much of the flour as you can with the mixer. Stir in any remaining flour with a wooden spoon. Stir in the oats and chocolate, and/or raisins, and/or dried fruit.

■ Drop dough by rounded tablespoons 3 inches apart onto ungreased cookie sheets. Bake in a preheated 375° oven for 12 to 15 minutes, or till golden brown. Let cool on cookie sheets for 1 minute. Remove cookies and cool on wire racks.

■ To make each cookie sandwich, pack ice cream into a ⅓-cup measure and unmold it onto the flat side of a cookie. Top with a second cookie, flat-side down. Press cookies together to secure. Wrap each sandwich in plastic wrap; freeze for about 1 hour, or till ice cream is solid.

Makes about 13 cookie sandwiches

Per cookie sandwich: 411 calories, 5 g protein, 50 g carbohydrate, 22 g total fat (12 g saturated), 84 mg cholesterol, 264 mg sodium, 199 mg potassium

Preparation Time: 20 minutes
Baking Time: 12 to 15 minutes
Freezing Time: 1 hour

STEPS AT A GLANCE	Page
SNIPPING FRUIT	21
MAKING COOKIE DOUGH	8
MAKING DROP COOKIES	14
MAKING "SANDWICHES"	22

STEPS FOR MAKING "SANDWICHES"

STEP 1 MOLDING ICE CREAM

Spoon ice cream into a ⅓-cup measure. Pack down so the ice cream forms a solid disk without air holes.

STEP 2 MAKING SANDWICHES

Unmold ice cream onto the flat bottom of a cookie. Top ice cream with another cookie, flat-side down.

STEP 3 WRAPPING COOKIES

Tightly wrap each sandwich in plastic wrap. Store in an airtight container and freeze until solid.

Ice Cream Sandwiches are a two-for-one dessert: your favorite ice cream plus a double serving of oatmeal cookies rich with your choice of chocolate pieces, raisins, and/or dried fruit.

Triple-Chocolate Cookies

STEPS AT A GLANCE	Page
MELTING CHOCOLATE	10
MAKING COOKIE DOUGH	8
MAKING DROP COOKIES	14

Preparation Time: 20 minutes
Baking Time: 8 to 10 minutes

INGREDIENTS

1/2	CUP SHORTENING
1/2	CUP BUTTER *OR* MARGARINE, SOFTENED
3/4	CUP GRANULATED SUGAR
3/4	CUP PACKED BROWN SUGAR
1	TEASPOON BAKING SODA
2	EGGS
1	TEASPOON VANILLA
2	OUNCES UNSWEETENED CHOCOLATE, MELTED AND COOLED
1/4	CUP UNSWEETENED COCOA POWDER
2	CUPS ALL-PURPOSE FLOUR
8	OUNCES SEMISWEET CHOCOLATE *OR* WHITE BAKING BAR, BROKEN INTO CHUNKS, *OR* ONE 10-OUNCE PACKAGE WHITE BAKING PIECES

Three different kinds of chocolate in one great cookie! They'll have a more intense flavor if you use the best-quality chocolate you can find. Candy stores or gourmet food shops usually have a good selection.

■ In a large mixing bowl beat the shortening and butter or margarine with an electric mixer on medium to high speed for 30 seconds. Add the granulated sugar, brown sugar, and baking soda; beat till combined. Beat in the eggs, vanilla, and melted chocolate. Beat in the cocoa powder and as much of the flour as you can with the mixer. Stir in any remaining flour with a wooden spoon. Stir in the semisweet chocolate, white baking bar, or white baking pieces.

■ Drop rounded tablespoons of dough 2 inches apart onto ungreased cookie sheets. Bake in a preheated 375° oven for 8 to 10 minutes, or till tops look dry. Cool on cookie sheets for 1 minute; remove cookies and cool on wire racks.

Makes about 48 cookies

Per cookie: 111 calories, 1 g protein, 13 g carbohydrate, 6 g total fat (3 g saturated), 14 mg cholesterol, 51 mg sodium, 50 mg potassium

For chocoholics everywhere, here's a triple-threat drop cookie that is chocolate, chocolate, and more chocolate.

Espresso Meringue Kisses

Preparation Time: 45 minutes
Baking Time: 15 to 20 minutes

A delicate web of chocolate criss-crosses espresso-flavored meringues.

INGREDIENTS

KISSES

2	EGG WHITES
3/4	CUP GRANULATED SUGAR
1	TEASPOON INSTANT ESPRESSO POWDER
1	TEASPOON VANILLA

CHOCOLATE GANACHE

1/3	CUP WHIPPING CREAM
2	TEASPOONS GRANULATED SUGAR
2	TEASPOONS BUTTER *OR* MARGARINE
3/4	CUP SEMISWEET CHOCOLATE PIECES

Espresso imparts a distinct coffee flavor to the meringue base of these soft, chewy cookies.

■ For kisses, in a medium mixing bowl let egg whites stand at room temperature for 30 minutes. Meanwhile, line 2 cookie sheets with parchment paper or brown kraft paper. Set aside. Stir together the sugar and espresso powder. Add vanilla to egg whites. Beat with an electric mixer on medium speed until soft peaks form (tips curl). Gradually add the sugar-espresso powder mixture, 1 tablespoon at a time, beating on high speed just till stiff peaks form (tips stand straight) and sugar is almost dissolved.

■ Drop mixture by slightly rounded teaspoons 2 inches apart onto prepared cookie sheets. Bake in a preheated 325° oven for 15 to 20 minutes, or till lightly browned. Remove cookies and cool on wire racks.

■ Meanwhile, for chocolate ganache, in a heavy saucepan stir together the whipping cream, sugar, and butter or margarine. Cook and stir over medium-high heat till sugar is dissolved. Bring mixture to boiling. Meanwhile, place chocolate pieces in a bowl; pour boiling cream mixture over chocolate. Let stand for 5 minutes; stir till smooth. Drizzle cookies with chocolate ganache just before serving. (Ganache may be refrigerated for up to several days. When ready to use, reheat ganache in a small saucepan over low heat, stirring constantly, till smooth and of drizzling consistency.)

Makes about 48 cookies

Per cookie: 21 calories, 0 g protein, 3 g carbohydrate, 1 g total fat (1 g saturated), 3 mg cholesterol, 5 mg sodium, 6 mg potassium

STEPS AT A GLANCE	Page
LINING COOKIE SHEET	18
MAKING MERINGUE	11
MAKING DROP COOKIES	14
DRIZZLING ICING OR CHOCOLATE	11

Orange-Fig Drops

A drizzle of orange icing provides a subtle contrast to fruit-filled golden cookies.

Preparation Time: 20 minutes
Baking Time: 10 to 12 minutes

INGREDIENTS

COOKIES

1/2	CUP SHORTENING
1	TEASPOON GROUND CINNAMON
1	TEASPOON FINELY SHREDDED ORANGE PEEL
1/2	TEASPOON BAKING SODA
1	EGG
1/2	CUP HONEY
3	TABLESPOONS ORANGE JUICE *OR* MILK
2	CUPS ALL-PURPOSE FLOUR
1	CUP SNIPPED DRIED FIGS *OR* PITTED DATES, *OR* RAISINS

ORANGE ICING

1	CUP SIFTED POWDERED SUGAR
1	TO 2 TABLESPOONS ORANGE JUICE

This recipe includes several alternate ingredients. Create your own version by using a mixture of dried fruits, or use apple juice in place of orange juice or milk.

STEPS AT A GLANCE	Page
SNIPPING FRUIT	21
MAKING COOKIE DOUGH	8
MAKING DROP COOKIES	14
DRIZZLING ICING OR CHOCOLATE	11

■ For cookies, in a mixing bowl beat shortening with an electric mixer on medium to high speed for 30 seconds. Add the cinnamon, orange peel, and baking soda; beat till combined. Beat in the egg, honey, and orange juice or milk till combined. Beat in as much of the flour as you can with the mixer. Stir in any remaining flour with a wooden spoon. Stir in figs, dates, or raisins.

■ Drop dough by rounded teaspoons 2 inches apart onto ungreased cookie sheets. Bake in a preheated 350° oven for 10 to 12 minutes, or till lightly browned. Remove cookies and cool on wire racks.

■ Meanwhile, for orange icing, in a small mixing bowl stir together powdered sugar and enough of the orange juice to make an icing of drizzling consistency. Drizzle cookies with icing.

Makes about 36 cookies

Per cookie: 91 calories, 1 g protein, 15 g carbohydrate, 3 g total fat (1 g saturated), 6 mg cholesterol, 19 mg sodium, 54 mg potassium

Carrot-Raisin Drops

INGREDIENTS

1	CUP BUTTER *OR* MARGARINE, SOFTENED
1	CUP PACKED BROWN SUGAR
1	TEASPOON BAKING SODA
1	TEASPOON GROUND CINNAMON
1	TEASPOON FINELY SHREDDED ORANGE PEEL
1/2	TEASPOON GROUND GINGER
1/2	TEASPOON GROUND NUTMEG
2	EGGS
1	TEASPOON VANILLA
1-1/2	CUPS ALL-PURPOSE FLOUR
1-1/2	CUPS FINELY SHREDDED CARROTS
1	CUP ROLLED OATS
1	CUP RAISINS
1/2	CUP CHOPPED WALNUTS *OR* PECANS

Preparation Time: 20 minutes
Baking Time: 6 to 8 minutes

STEPS AT A GLANCE	Page
MAKING COOKIE DOUGH	8
MAKING DROP COOKIES	14

If you want the flavor of carrot cake without the fuss, try these moist, cakelike cookies. And if you still want something sweet on top, spread each cookie with a little of your favorite cream cheese frosting recipe.

■ In a mixing bowl beat the butter or margarine with an electric mixer on medium to high speed for 30 seconds. Add the brown sugar, baking soda, cinnamon, orange peel, ginger, and nutmeg; beat till combined. Beat in the eggs and vanilla. Beat in as much of the flour as you can with the mixer. Stir in any remaining flour with a wooden spoon. Stir in the carrots, oats, raisins, and nuts.

■ Drop dough by rounded teaspoons 2 inches apart onto ungreased cookie sheets. Bake in a preheated 375° oven for 6 to 8 minutes, or till golden brown. Remove cookies and cool on wire racks.

Makes about 72 cookies

Per cookie: 63 calories, 1 g protein, 8 g carbohydrate, 3 g total fat (2 g saturated), 13 mg cholesterol, 51 mg sodium, 48 mg potassium

Golden-brown cookie nuggets get added sweetness from wholesome raisins and vitamin-rich carrots.

Coconut-Macadamia Cookies

Although pecans or almonds are delicious additions to these cookies, there really is no substitute for the mild, buttery taste of macadamias. They usually cost a little more, but we think they're worth it.

■ In a mixing bowl beat the butter or margarine with an electric mixer on medium to high speed for 30 seconds. Add the sugar and baking soda; beat till combined. Beat in the eggs, sour cream, and vanilla. Beat in as much of the flour as you can with the mixer. Stir in any remaining flour with a wooden spoon. Stir in the coconut and nuts.

■ Drop dough by rounded teaspoons 2 inches apart onto ungreased cookie sheets. Bake in a preheated 350° oven for about 10 to 12 minutes, or till golden brown. Remove cookies and cool on wire racks.

Makes about 72 cookies

Per cookie: 72 calories, 1 g protein, 7 g carbohydrate, 5 g total fat (2 g saturated), 10 mg cholesterol, 26 mg sodium, 25 mg potassium

INGREDIENTS

1/2	CUP BUTTER *OR* MARGARINE, SOFTENED
1	CUP GRANULATED SUGAR
1/2	TEASPOON BAKING SODA
2	EGGS
1/2	CUP DAIRY SOUR CREAM
1	TEASPOON VANILLA
2-1/2	CUPS ALL-PURPOSE FLOUR
2	CUPS COCONUT
1-1/2	CUPS CHOPPED MACADAMIA NUTS, PECANS, *OR* ALMONDS

Preparation Time: 20 minutes
Baking Time: 10 to 12 minutes

STEPS AT A GLANCE	Page
MAKING COOKIE DOUGH	8
MAKING DROP COOKIES	14

Exotic macadamia nuts and chewy coconut give a tropical accent to easy-to-make drop cookies, while sour cream gives them a slight tang.

Peanut Butter Brickle Drops

Bits of toffee brickle make chewy peanut butter drops extra chunky.

STEPS AT A GLANCE	Page
MAKING COOKIE DOUGH	8
MAKING DROP COOKIES	14

Preparation Time: 20 minutes
Baking Time: 8 to 10 minutes

INGREDIENTS

1	CUP BUTTER *OR* MARGARINE, SOFTENED
1-1/4	CUPS PACKED BROWN SUGAR
1/2	CUP GRANULATED SUGAR
1/2	TEASPOON BAKING SODA
2	EGGS
1	CUP CHUNKY PEANUT BUTTER
1	TEASPOON VANILLA
2-1/4	CUPS ALL-PURPOSE FLOUR
1	7-1/2-OUNCE PACKAGE ALMOND BRICKLE PIECES (1-1/3 CUPS)

If you love peanut butter cookies, try this delicious variation. The brickle pieces add a terrific crunchy-chewy texture to an old favorite.

■ In a large mixing bowl beat the butter or margarine with an electric mixer on medium to high speed for 30 seconds. Add the brown sugar, granulated sugar, and baking soda; beat till combined. Beat in the eggs, peanut butter, and vanilla. Beat in as much of the flour as you can with the mixer. Stir in any remaining flour with a wooden spoon. Stir in almond brickle pieces.

■ Drop dough by rounded teaspoons 2 inches apart onto ungreased cookie sheets. Bake in a preheated 375° oven for 8 to 10 minutes, or till golden brown. Remove cookies and cool on wire racks.

Makes about 64 cookies

Per cookie: 106 calories, 2 g protein, 12 g carbohydrate, 6 g total fat (2 g saturated), 16 mg cholesterol, 84 mg sodium, 53 mg potassium

Frosted Lime Wafers

Finely shredded lime peel and lime juice impart an aromatic, citrusy note to these delicate cookie wafers, which also may be made with lemons or oranges. Use only the thin colored peel of these fruits, not the bitter white pith beneath.

■ For wafers, in a mixing bowl beat the butter or margarine with an electric mixer on medium to high speed for 30 seconds. Add the sugar, baking soda, and lime or lemon peel; beat till combined. Beat in the lime or lemon juice. Beat in as much of the flour as you can with the mixer. Stir in any remaining flour with a wooden spoon.

■ Drop dough by rounded teaspoons 2 inches apart onto ungreased cookie sheets. Bake in a preheated 375° oven for about 10 minutes, or till the edges are beginning to brown. Remove cookies and cool on wire racks.

■ Meanwhile, for pastel glaze, in a small mixing bowl stir together the powdered sugar, melted butter or margarine, and enough lime or lemon juice to make a mixture of glazing consistency. If desired, stir in food coloring. Dip tops of cookies in glaze.

Makes about 48 cookies

Per cookie: 84 calories, 1 g protein, 10 g carbohydrate, 5 g total fat (3 g saturated), 12 mg cholesterol, 66 mg sodium, 10 mg potassium

Tart, lime-infused wafers team up with fruit sherbet for a refreshing warm-weather dessert.

STEPS AT A GLANCE	Page
MAKING COOKIE DOUGH	8
MAKING DROP COOKIES	14

Preparation Time: 20 minutes
Baking Time: 10 minutes

INGREDIENTS

WAFERS

1	CUP BUTTER *OR* MARGARINE, SOFTENED
1	CUP GRANULATED SUGAR
1/2	TEASPOON BAKING SODA
1/2	TEASPOON FINELY SHREDDED LIME PEEL *OR* 1 TEASPOON FINELY SHREDDED LEMON PEEL
1/3	CUP LIME JUICE *OR* LEMON JUICE
2-1/4	CUPS ALL-PURPOSE FLOUR

PASTEL GLAZE

1	CUP SIFTED POWDERED SUGAR
3	TABLESPOONS BUTTER *OR* MARGARINE, MELTED
1	TO 2 TABLESPOONS LIME JUICE *OR* LEMON JUICE
	FEW DROPS GREEN *OR* YELLOW FOOD COLORING (OPTIONAL)

Bar Cookies

Steps for Making Bar Cookies

SAUCEPAN

BAKING PAN

BOWL

RUBBER SPATULA

WOODEN SPOON

BASIC TOOLS FOR MAKING BAR COOKIES

Some bar cookie recipes are so simple that the batter is mixed in a saucepan, then spooned right into a baking pan.

MIX, BAKE, SERVE. Bar cookies are that basic. But here *basic* means extremely easy, not bland or boring. Brownies (like the delectable mocha-flavored ones opposite) fall into this category, and it's hard to imagine a more delicious dessert or one with a bigger fan club. Unlike drop cookies, which use a soft dough, bar cookies are made with a fluid batter that needs a baking pan with sides for support. For best results, spread the batter evenly in the pan, so that the finished bars aren't thin and dried out in one corner and thick and underdone in another. Let the bars cool in the pan, then cut into uniform portions such as squares, rectangles, triangles, or diamonds (see page 35 for complete directions for these steps). To remove for serving or storage, first run a sharp, thin-bladed knife between the bars and the inside edge of the pan, then lift them out with a spatula that is large enough to fully support each piece.

too much shortening will make the bars gummy; too little will cause them to stick to the pan

STEP 1 PREPARING PAN

If the baking pan must be greased, do it as the first step in the recipe. Coat a piece of paper towel or waxed paper with shortening, then apply in a thin, even layer on the bottom and sides of the pan.

STEP 2 COMBINING INGREDIENTS

If the batter calls for a melted ingredient such as chocolate, let it cool slightly before beating in the eggs. Then gently stir in the remaining ingredients, such as flour and baking powder, with a wooden spoon.

STEP 3 SPREADING BATTER IN PAN

Spread the batter in a smooth, even layer across the pan bottom with a rubber spatula or the back of a wooden spoon. If the pan has sharp corners, as does this one, make sure the batter fills each one completely.

STEP 4 TESTING FOR DONENESS

Toward the end of baking time, begin to check for doneness. Depending on the recipe, look for the batter to be set, for the edges to be slightly browned, or for the mixture to pull away slightly from the sides of the pan.

Use a metal icing spatula or the back of a spoon to texture frosting into decorative swirls and ridges. The recipe for Mocha Brownies, shown here, is on page 42.

Steps for Making Bar Cookies with a Crust

BASIC TOOLS FOR MAKING BAR COOKIES WITH A CRUST

Use a mixing bowl and pastry blender to prepare cookie crusts, a rubber spatula to transfer batter to a baking pan and to spread fillings, and a sharp knife and toothpicks to cut even bars.

BAKING PAN AND COOLING RACK

MIXING BOWL

PASTRY BLENDER

SMALL, SHARP KNIFE

RUBBER SPATULA

TOOTHPICKS

MULTILAYERED BAR cookies have great visual appeal. Although they look complex, they are simple to assemble, which means maximum results for minimum effort. Most bar cookie crusts are quickly tossed together with a pastry blender or a spoon and formed into a layer in the pan with your fingers like press-in pie pastry. The end result might be a rich dough that resembles the base for Coffee-Pecan Triangles (page 45) or one made with cookie crumbs like the crust of Orange Cheesecake Dreams (page 37). If the filling is very liquid, the crust will be prebaked so it won't get soggy. When cutting bar cookies and bar cookies with a crust, you will get the neatest results if you mark off your lines with a simple grid. Use toothpicks as guides for your cutting lines for either squares or diamonds. A perfect square cut in half yields a perfect triangle. For a more generous triangular shape, cut rectangles in half (see page 44).

if the pastry blender gets clogged with butter or margarine, clean it with a rubber spatula or your finger

STEP 1 CUTTING IN BUTTER OR MARGARINE
Use a fork to stir together flour, sugar, and salt until thoroughly blended. Cut cold butter or margarine into pieces and cut in with a pastry blender, using an up-and-down motion, until the mixture is crumbly.

STEP 2 PRESSING INTO PAN

Transfer the crust mixture to a baking pan (with a rich dough there is no need to grease the pan first). Push the dough around with your hands until it covers the bottom of the pan in an even layer. Be sure to fill the corners.

STEP 3 SPREADING FILLING EVENLY

While the crust bakes briefly, prepare the filling. Remove the crust from the oven, set it on a cooling rack, and pour on the filling. Spread it evenly with a rubber spatula so that every part of the hot crust is covered.

STEP 4 CUTTING BAR COOKIES

Let the cookies cool completely in the pan before cutting them. Then mark cutting lines with toothpicks inserted around the inside edge of the pan. Cut the cookies with a small, sharp knife, using the toothpicks as guides.

STEP 5 CUTTING TRIANGLES

Make cookie squares according to the directions in step 4; leave them in the pan. To create triangles, cut each square in half diagonally, working from one side of the pan to the other.

STEP 6 CUTTING DIAMONDS

As in step 4, place toothpicks around the rim of the pan to mark where you will cut. Divide the cookie lengthwise into long strips, then cut the strips into diamonds by making diagonal cuts from one side of the pan to the other.

Cut bar cookies into simple shapes like squares or triangles after baking. These Coffee-Pecan Triangles appear on page 45.

Orange peel and orange juice add a refreshing note to creamy bars. Serve them as the cool finale to a spicy meal.

Orange Cheesecake Dreams

A light orange flavor gives these individual cheesecakes an unexpected tang. If you're making them for company, garnish each square with a thin half slice of orange.

■ For crust, in a medium mixing bowl stir together the vanilla wafer crumbs and melted butter or margarine. Set aside ½ cup of the crumb mixture. Press remaining mixture evenly into the bottom of a 13x9x2-inch baking pan. Bake in a preheated 350° oven for 15 minutes.

■ For filling, in another mixing bowl beat cream cheese with an electric mixer on medium to high speed for 30 seconds. Beat in sugar and orange peel till combined. Beat in eggs and orange juice on low speed just till combined. Do not overbeat. Spread cream cheese mixture evenly over crust. Sprinkle with reserved crumb mixture.

■ Bake in the 350° oven for 30 to 35 minutes, or till center appears set. Cool in pan on a rack. Cut into bars; cover and store in the refrigerator.

Makes about 36 bars

Per bar: 88 calories, 1 g protein, 8 g carbohydrate, 6 g total fat (3 g saturated), 29 mg cholesterol, 61 mg sodium, 22 mg potassium

STEPS AT A GLANCE	Page
MAKING CRUMB TOPPING	37
MAKING BAR COOKIES WITH A CRUST	34

Preparation Time: 25 minutes
Baking Time: 45 to 50 minutes

INGREDIENTS

CRUST

- 2 CUPS FINELY CRUSHED VANILLA WAFERS (ABOUT 44 WAFERS)
- 1/3 CUP BUTTER *OR* MARGARINE, MELTED

FILLING

- 1 8-OUNCE PACKAGE CREAM CHEESE, SOFTENED
- 1 3-OUNCE PACKAGE CREAM CHEESE, SOFTENED
- 3/4 CUP GRANULATED SUGAR
- 2 TEASPOONS FINELY SHREDDED ORANGE PEEL
- 2 EGGS
- 1/3 CUP ORANGE JUICE

STEPS FOR MAKING CRUMB TOPPING

STEP 1 CRUSHING WAFERS
Place vanilla wafers in a heavy-duty plastic bag. Press out all of the air, then seal the bag. Crush the cookies into crumbs by rolling over them with a rolling pin.

STEP 2 SPRINKLING CRUMBS
Spread the cream cheese filling evenly over the partially baked wafer crust with a rubber spatula. Sprinkle the reserved crumb mixture evenly over the filling.

Chocolate-Raspberry Brownies

INGREDIENTS

BROWNIES

- 1/2 CUP BUTTER *OR* MARGARINE
- 2 OUNCES UNSWEETENED CHOCOLATE
- 1 CUP GRANULATED SUGAR
- 2 EGGS
- 1 TEASPOON VANILLA
- 1/2 TEASPOON ALMOND EXTRACT
- 1 CUP ALL-PURPOSE FLOUR
- 1/3 CUP SEEDLESS RASPBERRY JAM *OR* PRESERVES

COCOA FROSTING

- 1-1/2 CUPS SIFTED POWDERED SUGAR
- 3 TABLESPOONS UNSWEETENED COCOA POWDER
- 3 TABLESPOONS BUTTER *OR* MARGARINE, MELTED
- 1 TEASPOON VANILLA
- 1 TO 2 TABLESPOONS BOILING WATER

Raspberry and chocolate are a classic pairing, but other flavors of preserves like cherry, for example, are equally luscious in this recipe.

■ For brownies, in a medium saucepan melt butter or margarine and chocolate over low heat, stirring frequently. Remove from heat. Add the sugar, eggs, vanilla, and almond extract. Using a wooden spoon, lightly beat in flour just till combined. (Do not overbeat or brownies will fall when baked.)

■ Spread batter into a greased 8x8x2-inch baking pan. Spoon raspberry jam in dollops over batter; run a knife through batter several times to achieve a marbled effect. Bake in a preheated 350° oven for about 35 minutes, or till set. Cool in pan on a rack.

■ Meanwhile, for cocoa frosting, in a medium mixing bowl stir together the powdered sugar, cocoa powder, melted butter or margarine, and vanilla. Stir in enough of the boiling water to make a frosting of spreading consistency. Spread over cooled brownies. If desired, score frosting with the tines of a fork. Cut into bars.

Makes about 20 brownies

Per brownie: 187 calories, 2 g protein, 27 g carbohydrate, 8 g total fat (5 g saturated), 39 mg cholesterol, 81 mg sodium, 45 mg potassium

Preparation Time: 15 minutes
Baking Time: 35 minutes

STEPS AT A GLANCE	Page
MAKING BAR COOKIES	32
MAKING SWIRLED TOPPING & FROSTING	38

STEPS FOR MAKING SWIRLED TOPPING AND FROSTING

STEP 1 ADDING PRESERVES

Prepare the batter and spread in the greased baking pan. Spoon seedless raspberry preserves at even intervals across the surface.

STEP 2 MARBLING PRESERVES

Insert a small metal spatula or knife in the center of one spoonful of preserves. Drag through the preserves with a swirling motion to pull them through the batter until you reach another dollop of preserves. Continue swirling the remaining preserves to create a marbleized pattern.

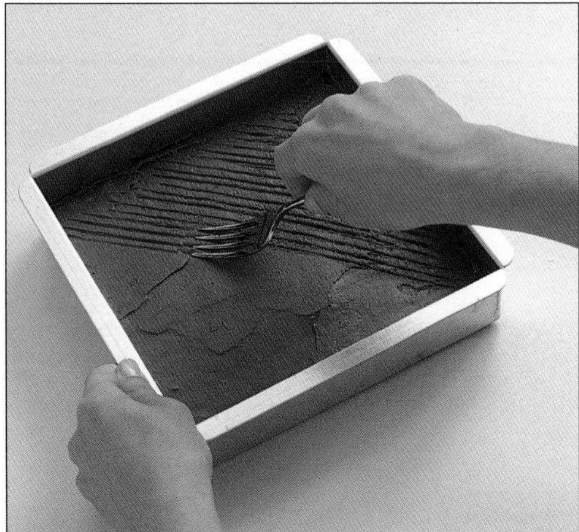

STEP 3 SCORING FROSTING

Spread frosting evenly over the entire surface of the batter. Using just enough pressure to make score marks, pull the tines of a fork through the frosting on the diagonal.

Raspberry preserves swirl through a rich chocolate brownie bar that complements after-dinner coffee.

Not only were these bars inspired by toffee candy, they use candy bars to make a simple chocolate frosting.

Hazelnut Toffee Bars

These toffee confections are like melt-in-your-mouth homemade candy bars. Sprinkle broken toffee candy bar or brickle bits over the top instead of nuts for a decadent touch.

■ In a medium mixing bowl beat the butter or margarine with an electric mixer on medium to high speed for 30 seconds. Add the brown sugar and salt and beat till combined. Beat in the milk and vanilla. Beat in as much of the flour as you can with the mixer. Stir in any remaining flour with a wooden spoon. Stir in half of the hazelnuts, pecans, or walnuts.

■ Spread batter in a greased 13x9x2-inch baking pan. Bake in a preheated 350° oven for 20 to 25 minutes, or till lightly browned around the edges.

■ Immediately place candy bars on top of the hot crust. Let stand for 2 to 3 minutes, or till chocolate is melted. Spread chocolate evenly over crust. Sprinkle remaining nuts over chocolate. Cool in pan on a rack. Cut into bars.

Makes about 36 bars

Per bar: 133 calories, 2 g protein, 11 g carbohydrate, 9 g total fat (5 g saturated), 14 mg cholesterol, 100 mg sodium, 63 mg potassium

STEPS AT A GLANCE	Page
MAKING BAR COOKIES	32
MAKING MELTED TOPPING	41

Preparation Time: 20 minutes
Baking Time: 20 to 25 minutes

INGREDIENTS

1	CUP BUTTER *OR* MARGARINE, SOFTENED
1/2	CUP PACKED BROWN SUGAR
1/2	TEASPOON SALT
3	TABLESPOONS MILK
1	TEASPOON VANILLA
1-1/2	CUPS ALL-PURPOSE FLOUR
1	CUP FINELY CHOPPED HAZELNUTS, PECANS, *OR* WALNUTS
6	1-1/2-OUNCE MILK CHOCOLATE CANDY BARS

STEPS FOR MAKING MELTED TOPPING

STEP 1 ADDING CANDY
Bake the cookie crust until lightly browned around the edges and remove from the oven. Immediately arrange unwrapped milk-chocolate candy bars in two even rows over the hot crust.

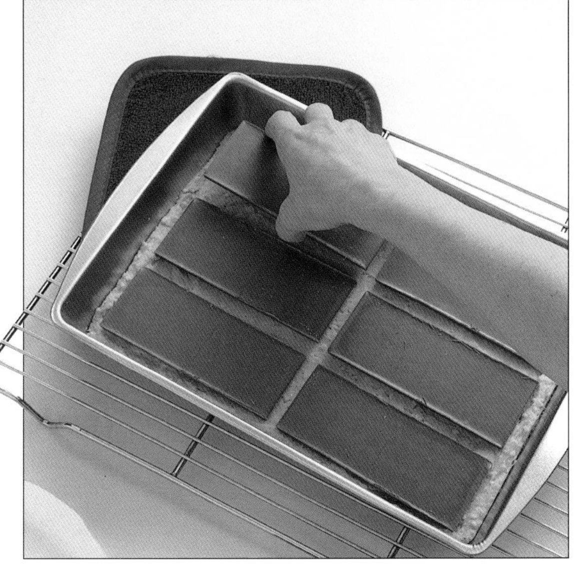

STEP 2 SPREADING CANDY
Wait for the chocolate to melt, then spread the melted bars over the cookie crust with an icing knife or small spatula, making some swirls and ridges for texture.

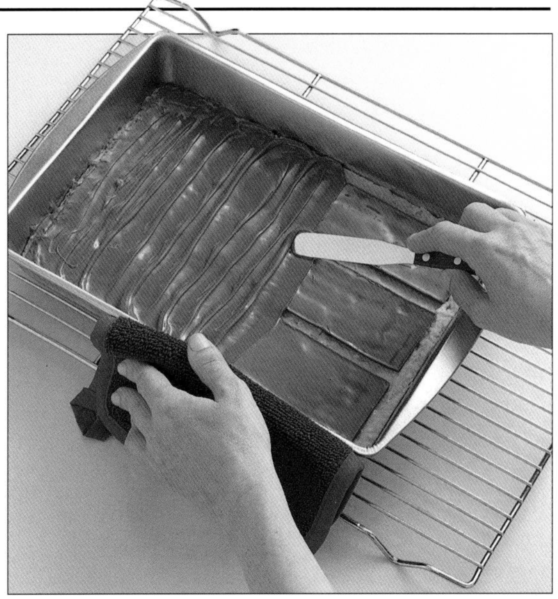

Mocha Brownies

Preparation Time: 20 minutes
Baking Time: 25 minutes

Coffee and chocolate always enhance each other. Mocha Brownies are the delicious proof.

INGREDIENTS

BROWNIES

1	CUP GRANULATED SUGAR
1/2	CUP BUTTER *OR* MARGARINE
1/3	CUP UNSWEETENED COCOA POWDER
1	TEASPOON INSTANT COFFEE CRYSTALS
2	EGGS
1	TEASPOON VANILLA
2/3	CUP ALL-PURPOSE FLOUR
1/2	TEASPOON BAKING POWDER
1/4	TEASPOON SALT
1/2	CUP CHOPPED WALNUTS

FROSTING

3	TABLESPOONS BUTTER *OR* MARGARINE, SOFTENED
1/4	CUP UNSWEETENED COCOA POWDER
2	CUPS SIFTED POWDERED SUGAR
2	TO 3 TABLESPOONS MILK
1/2	TEASPOON VANILLA

These saucepan brownies are easy to mix up when unexpected guests arrive, and they're the perfect base for brownie sundaes, just like Blonde Brownies (opposite page).

■ For brownies, in a medium saucepan combine granulated sugar, butter or margarine, cocoa powder, and coffee crystals. Cook and stir over medium heat till butter or margarine melts. Remove from heat; cool for 5 minutes. Add eggs and vanilla. Beat lightly by hand just till combined. Stir in the flour, baking powder, and salt. Stir in walnuts. Spread the batter in a greased 9x9x2-inch baking pan. Bake in a preheated 350° oven for 25 minutes, or till set. Cool in pan on a rack.

■ For frosting, in a mixing bowl beat butter or margarine till fluffy. Add cocoa powder. Gradually add 1 cup of the powdered sugar, beating well. Slowly beat in 2 tablespoons of the milk and the vanilla. Slowly beat in remaining sugar. Beat in additional milk, if necessary, to make a frosting of spreading consistency.

■ Spread frosting over cooled brownies. Cut into bars.

Makes about 12 brownies

Per brownie: 308 calories, 4 g protein, 41 g carbohydrate, 15 g fat (7 g saturated), 64 mg cholesterol, 164 mg sodium, 58 mg potassium

STEPS AT A GLANCE	Page
MAKING BAR COOKIES	32

Blonde Brownies

If you're feeling self-indulgent, these brownies make a fantastic sundae when topped with ice cream, hot fudge, and some chopped nuts. Garnish with fresh fruit.

■ In a large saucepan heat brown sugar and butter or margarine, stirring constantly till sugar dissolves. Remove pan from heat. Cool slightly. Add eggs, one at a time, and the vanilla. Beat slightly by hand just till combined. Stir in flour, baking powder, and baking soda.

■ Spread batter in a greased 13x9x2-inch baking pan. Sprinkle with chopped chocolate and hazelnuts or almonds.

■ Bake in a preheated 350° oven for 35 minutes. Cut into bars while still warm; cool bars completely in pan.

Makes about 36 brownies

Per brownie: 142 calories, 1 g protein, 20 g carbohydrate, 7 g total fat (3 g saturated), 21 mg cholesterol, 56 mg sodium, 77 mg potassium

INGREDIENTS

2	CUPS PACKED BROWN SUGAR
2/3	CUP BUTTER *OR* MARGARINE
2	EGGS
2	TEASPOONS VANILLA
2	CUPS ALL-PURPOSE FLOUR
1	TEASPOON BAKING POWDER
1/4	TEASPOON BAKING SODA
1	CUP CHOPPED SWEET BAKING CHOCOLATE (6 OUNCES)
2/3	CUP TOASTED CHOPPED HAZELNUTS *OR* ALMONDS

Preparation Time: 20 minutes
Baking Time: 35 minutes

STEPS AT A GLANCE	Page
TOASTING NUTS	11
MAKING BAR COOKIES	32

These chewy golden bars will remind you of a thick chocolate chip cookie made with chopped chocolate and toasted nuts.

Sour Cream–Date Triangles

Fruit-and-nut triangles are aromatic with spices and the molasseslike flavor of brown sugar. They suit a dessert tray or brunch spread equally well and bring out the best in a steaming cup of tea.

STEPS AT A GLANCE	Page
MAKING BAR COOKIES	32

Preparation Time: 25 minutes
Baking Time: 20 to 25 minutes

INGREDIENTS

BARS

2	CUPS ALL-PURPOSE FLOUR
1-1/2	CUPS PACKED BROWN SUGAR
1	TEASPOON BAKING POWDER
1	TEASPOON GROUND CINNAMON
1/2	TEASPOON BAKING SODA
1/2	TEASPOON SALT
2	EGGS
1	CUP BUTTER *OR* MARGARINE, SOFTENED
1/2	CUP DAIRY SOUR CREAM
1	8-OUNCE PACKAGE CHOPPED PITTED DATES *OR* 1-1/3 CUPS RAISINS
1/2	CUP CHOPPED WALNUTS *OR* PECANS

GLAZE

1-1/2	CUPS SIFTED POWDERED SUGAR
3	TABLESPOONS BUTTER *OR* MARGARINE, MELTED
1	TABLESPOON LEMON JUICE
1	TO 2 TABLESPOONS WATER
	FEW DROPS YELLOW FOOD COLORING (OPTIONAL)

■ For bars, in a medium mixing bowl stir together the flour, brown sugar, baking powder, cinnamon, baking soda, and salt. Beat in the eggs, butter or margarine, and sour cream till thoroughly combined. Stir in the dates or raisins and walnuts or pecans. Spread the batter in a greased 15x10x1-inch baking pan.

■ Bake in a preheated 350° oven for 20 to 25 minutes, or till a wooden toothpick inserted near the center comes out clean. Cool in pan on a rack.

■ For glaze, in a medium mixing bowl stir together the powdered sugar, melted butter or margarine, lemon juice, and enough water to make a mixture of glazing consistency. If desired, tint glaze with food coloring. Spread glaze over cooled bars. Cut into rectangles, then halve rectangles diagonally to make triangles.

Makes about 36 triangles

Per serving: 164 calories, 2 g protein, 23 g carbohydrate, 8 g total fat (4 g saturated), 29 mg cholesterol, 117 mg sodium, 99 mg potassium

A translucent lemony glaze covers rich, spicy fruit-filled bar cookies cut into generous triangles.

Coffee-Pecan Triangles

STEPS AT A GLANCE	Page
MAKING BAR COOKIES WITH A CRUST	34

Preparation Time: 25 minutes
Baking Time: 30 minutes

INGREDIENTS

CRUST

2	CUPS ALL-PURPOSE FLOUR
1/2	CUP SIFTED POWDERED SUGAR
1/2	TEASPOON SALT
3/4	CUP COLD BUTTER *OR* MARGARINE

FILLING

2	EGGS
1/2	CUP PACKED BROWN SUGAR
1	CUP CHOPPED PECANS
1/2	CUP HONEY
1/4	CUP BUTTER *OR* MARGARINE, MELTED
2	TABLESPOONS HALF-AND-HALF *OR* LIGHT CREAM
1	TEASPOON INSTANT COFFEE CRYSTALS
1	TEASPOON VANILLA

These rich, creamy bars are a snap to make. Follow the instructions on page 35, step 5, to cut them into neat triangles.

■ For crust, in a medium mixing bowl stir together the flour, powdered sugar, and salt. Cut in butter or margarine till crumbly. Press mixture evenly into the bottom of a 13x9x2-inch baking pan. Bake in a preheated 350° oven for 10 minutes.

■ Meanwhile, for filling, in another mixing bowl beat eggs slightly. Stir in the brown sugar, pecans, honey, and melted butter or margarine. Stir together the half-and-half or light cream, coffee crystals, and vanilla till coffee crystals dissolve. Stir into pecan mixture. Spread mixture evenly over hot crust.

■ Bake in the 350° oven for 20 minutes more, or till set. Cool in pan on a rack. Cut into squares, then halve squares diagonally to make triangles.

Makes about 48 triangles

Per triangle: 94 calories, 1 g protein, 10 g carbohydrate, 6 g total fat (2 g saturated), 19 mg cholesterol, 72 mg sodium, 32 mg potassium

A meltingly tender cookie crust is hidden beneath a glossy nut-covered topping that turns a rich mahogany as it bakes.

Apricot Macaroon Bars

Dried apricots and coconut make these tender bars incredibly moist. The coconut on top is toasted for extra flavor.

Preparation Time: 30 minutes
Baking Time: 35 minutes

INGREDIENTS

CRUST

3/4	CUP BUTTER *OR* MARGARINE, SOFTENED
1	CUP GRANULATED SUGAR
2	EGGS
1/4	TEASPOON ALMOND EXTRACT
1-1/2	CUPS ALL-PURPOSE FLOUR
1	CUP COCONUT

FILLING

1	6-OUNCE PACKAGE DRIED APRICOTS, SNIPPED (1-1/2 CUPS)
1	CUP WATER
1/2	CUP PACKED BROWN SUGAR
1/2	TEASPOON VANILLA
1/3	CUP TOASTED COCONUT

Most apricot bars have a cookie crust, but these are a cross between a light coconut cake and macaroons. You can use other dried fruits for a different flavor.

■ For crust, in a large mixing bowl beat butter or margarine with an electric mixer on medium to high speed for 30 seconds. Add the granulated sugar and beat till combined. Beat in eggs and almond extract. Beat in as much of the flour as you can with the mixer. Stir in any remaining flour with a wooden spoon. Stir in coconut. Spread the batter into a well-greased 13x9x2-inch baking pan. Bake in a preheated 350° oven for 25 minutes.

■ Meanwhile, for filling, in a saucepan combine the dried apricots and water. Bring to boiling; reduce heat. Simmer, covered, for 7 to 8 minutes, or till apricots are tender. Stir in brown sugar. Cook and stir till sugar is dissolved. Remove from heat and stir in vanilla. Spoon over hot crust. Sprinkle evenly with toasted coconut.

■ Bake in the 350° oven for 10 minutes more, or till a toothpick inserted near the center comes out clean. Cool in pan on a rack. Cut into bars.

Makes about 36 bars

Per bar: 111 calories, 1 g protein, 16 g carbohydrate, 5 g total fat (3 g saturated), 22 mg cholesterol, 50 mg sodium, 95 mg potassium

STEPS AT A GLANCE	Page
SNIPPING FRUIT	21
MAKING BAR COOKIES WITH A CRUST	34

Pumpkin Spice Bars

STEPS AT A GLANCE	Page
MAKING BAR COOKIES	32
PIPING CHOCOLATE	17

Preparation Time: 25 minutes
Baking Time: 15 to 20 minutes

INGREDIENTS

BARS

1-1/2	CUPS ALL-PURPOSE FLOUR
1	CUP PACKED BROWN SUGAR
1/2	CUP GRANULATED SUGAR
2	TEASPOONS BAKING POWDER
1/4	TEASPOON BAKING SODA
2	TEASPOONS FINELY CHOPPED CRYSTALLIZED GINGER *OR* 1/2 TEASPOON GROUND GINGER
1	TEASPOON GROUND CINNAMON
1/4	TEASPOON SALT
2	EGGS
1	CUP CANNED PUMPKIN
3/4	CUP RAISINS
1/2	CUP COOKING OIL

TOPPING

3	OUNCES WHITE BAKING BAR, CHOPPED
1	TEASPOON SHORTENING

Don't wait until fall to make these cakelike bars; they're just as good with a glass of lemonade as with a cup of hot cider. Canned pumpkin is available in supermarkets throughout the year. Look for crystallized ginger in specialty stores.

■ For bars, in a large mixing bowl stir together the flour, brown sugar, granulated sugar, baking powder, baking soda, crystallized or ground ginger, cinnamon, and salt. In another mixing bowl beat the eggs slightly. Stir in the pumpkin, raisins, and oil. Stir pumpkin mixture into flour mixture.

■ Spread batter into an ungreased 15x10x1-inch baking pan. Bake in a preheated 350° oven for 15 to 20 minutes, or till a wooden toothpick inserted near the center comes out clean. Cool in pan on a rack.

■ For topping, in a small, heavy-duty plastic bag combine baking bar and shortening. Close bag just above ingredients, then set sealed bag in a bowl of warm water till contents are melted. Snip ¼ inch from one corner of bag. Squeeze topping from bag over bars in a crisscross design. Cut bars before topping is completely set.

Makes about 48 bars

Per bar: 81 calories, 1 g protein, 13 g carbohydrate, 3 g total fat (1 g saturated), 9 mg cholesterol, 22 mg sodium, 61 mg potassium

Create a lattice effect by piping the topping over the bars in diagonal lines, first in one direction, then the other.

Chocolate-Coconut Meringue Bars

STEPS AT A GLANCE	Page
MAKING BAR COOKIES	32
MAKING MERINGUE	11

Preparation Time: 25 minutes
Baking Time: 40 to 45 minutes

INGREDIENTS

BARS

- 3/4 CUP BUTTER *OR* MARGARINE
- 3 OUNCES SEMISWEET CHOCOLATE, CHOPPED
- 1 CUP PACKED BROWN SUGAR
- 2 EGG YOLKS
- 1 TEASPOON VANILLA
- 1-3/4 CUPS ALL-PURPOSE FLOUR
- 1/4 TEASPOON SALT
- 1 CUP COCONUT

MERINGUE

- 2 EGG WHITES
- 1/2 CUP GRANULATED SUGAR
- 1/2 CUP FINELY CHOPPED ALMONDS *OR* PECANS
- 2 TABLESPOONS COCONUT

The coconut and meringue add a crunchy dimension to the brownie crust. These are best eaten the first day, although they will keep overnight in the refrigerator.

■ For bars, in a medium, heavy saucepan heat butter or margarine and chocolate over medium heat till melted, stirring frequently. Stir in the brown sugar, egg yolks, and vanilla. Using a wooden spoon, beat lightly just till combined. (Do not overbeat or bars will fall when baked.) Stir in the flour, salt, and coconut. Spread batter in a greased 9x9x2-inch baking pan. Bake in a preheated 350° oven for 25 minutes.

■ Meanwhile, for meringue, in a medium mixing bowl beat the egg whites with an electric mixer on high speed till soft peaks form (tips curl). Gradually beat in the granulated sugar, 1 tablespoon at a time, till stiff peaks form (tips stand up) and sugar is almost dissolved. Spread over hot crust. Sprinkle with chopped almonds and coconut.

■ Bake in the 350° oven for 15 to 20 minutes more, or till meringue is set and lightly browned. Cool in pan on a rack. Cut into bars.

Makes about 16 bars

Per bar: 280 calories, 4 g protein, 35 g carbohydrate, 15 g total fat (8 g saturated), 50 mg cholesterol, 148 mg sodium, 142 mg potassium

The meringue layer is spread over the hot brownie crust, sprinkled with chopped nuts and coconut, and baked until set and golden.

Cutout Cookies

Steps for Making Cutout Cookies

BASIC TOOLS FOR MAKING CUTOUT COOKIES

Use a ruler to measure the thickness of rolled-out dough, then cut into shapes with sharp-edged cutters. Transfer cookies with a spatula to a cookie sheet to bake, then cool on a wire rack.

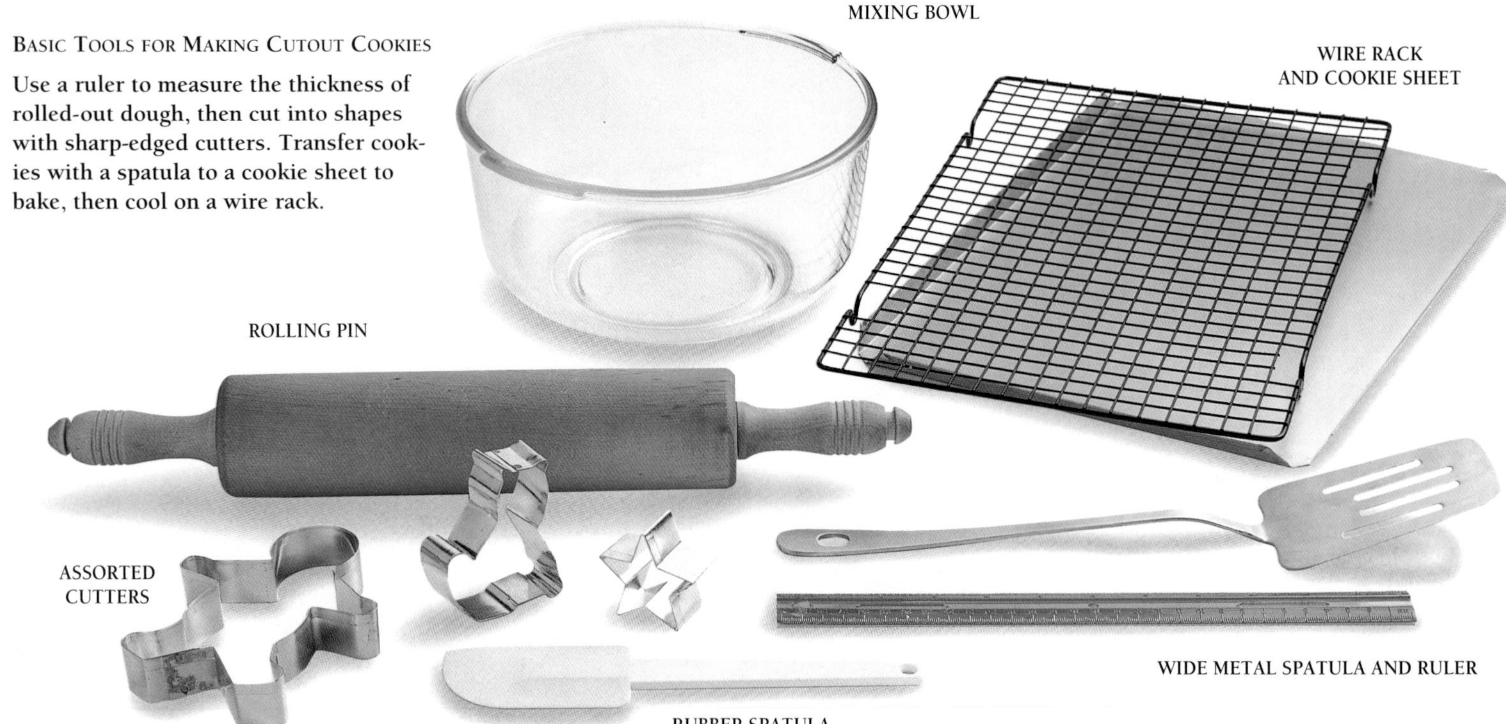

A BUTTERY COOKIE shaped like a little boy, or a cookie kitten with its tail tucked under, is more than just a confection. It is an edible example of cookie artistry. Some cutout cookies are formed with a cutter, some are created with a ruler and knife. All are made from a rich, pliable dough that must be chilled for easier handling, a plus because it can be made up to 1 week ahead. When ready, roll it out into a thin, even sheet. Then the fun begins: There are countless cookie cutter shapes for every occasion. Be sure to select cutters with sharp edges and patterns that are free of tiny details such as little ears or skinny tails that might break off as the dough drops from the cutter. To make the most out of a piece of dough, view it like an uncut puzzle and space the cutouts as close together as you can. Knead the scraps and reroll to use up the remaining dough. After baking, let the cookies cool briefly on the cookie sheet, then transfer to a wire cooling rack with a large spatula that will fully support each cookie. Let hot cookie sheets cool before using them again, or the cutouts will spread out of shape.

chilled dough is easier to roll and won't stick to the rolling pin

well-wrapped dough can be stored in the refrigerator for up to 1 week

STEP 1 CHILLING DOUGH

Prepare the dough and divide it into two equal pieces; flatten slightly. Tear off two large squares of plastic wrap. Tightly wrap each piece of dough in plastic wrap and chill until the dough is easy to handle, about 1 to 3 hours, depending on the recipe.

the thickness may differ depending on the recipe

STEP 2 Measuring Thickness

On a lightly floured surface, roll out one portion of dough ⅛ inch thick (keep the remaining half chilled until needed). Measure the dough with a ruler to check that it is of uniform thickness.

if desired, peel away the dough scraps around the cookie shapes first to make them easier to reach

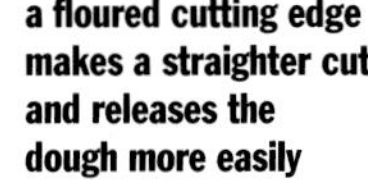

a floured cutting edge makes a straighter cut and releases the dough more easily

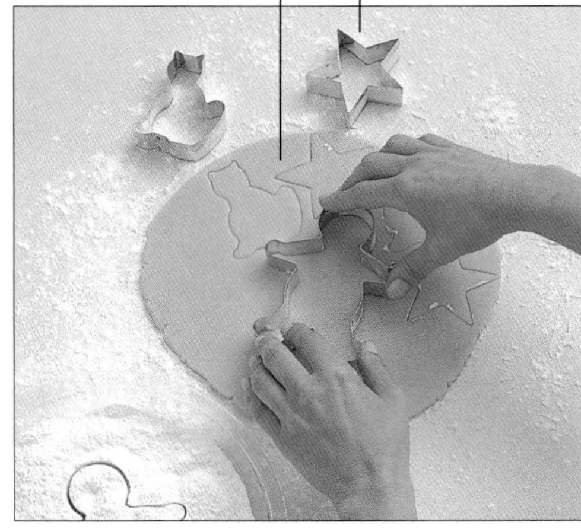

STEP 3 Cutting Out Cookies

Dip the cutting edge of the cookie cutter into flour. Set the cutter on the dough. Press straight down with equal pressure all the way around so that all parts of the pattern are cut out.

if the cookie sticks to the cutter, hold the cutter over the cookie sheet and gently tap one edge on the sheet to dislodge the dough

STEP 4 Moving Cookie to Sheet

Slide a large, wide spatula under the cookie and transfer it to a cookie sheet. Leave some room between the cutouts because they will expand as they bake.

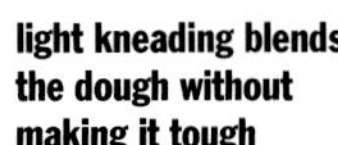

light kneading blends the dough without making it tough

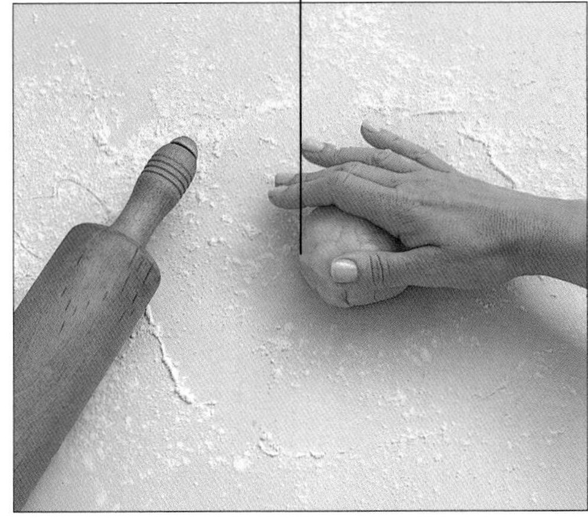

STEP 5 Rerolling Scraps

After as many cookies as possible have been cut out of the dough, gather the scraps with your lightly floured hands and gently knead the dough. Then reroll the dough ⅛ inch thick and cut out more cookies.

sugar cookies and most other cutouts brown lightly only on the bottom (the edges are firm, but not browned).

STEP 6 Testing for Doneness

If you think the cookies are ready to remove from the oven, check by lifting one with a spatula to see the color on its underside. Transfer to a wire rack to cool.

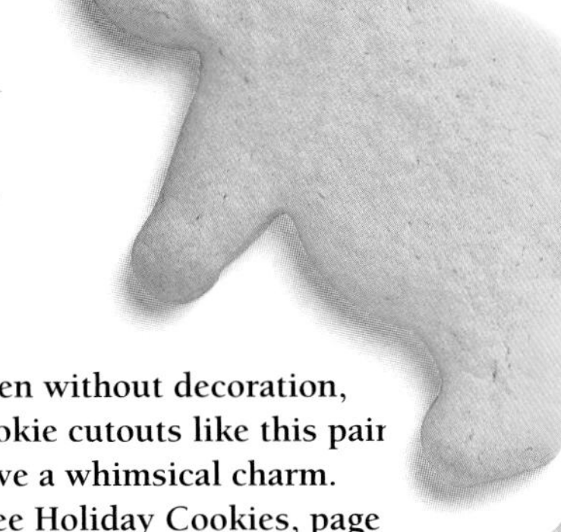

Even without decoration, cookie cutouts like this pair have a whimsical charm. (See Holiday Cookies, page 62, for the recipe.)

Steps for Making a Gingerbread Cottage

BASIC TOOLS FOR BUILDING COTTAGE

You will need the tools shown here, plus the items listed below, to build a gingerbread cottage.

MIXING BOWL AND SMALL BOWLS

CARDBOARD

BAKING SHEET

PARCHMENT PAPER OR CLEAN BROWN KRAFT PAPER

ELECTRIC MIXER

TOOTHPICKS

SHARP KNIFE

PENCIL

PASTRY BAG AND TIPS

ICING SPATULA

HORS D'OEUVRE CUTTERS

ATTENTION BUDDING ARCHITECTS: Design your dream house, guaranteed ready for immediate enjoyment! Gingerbread may not be the most permanent building material, but it is certainly the most delicious. For many families, baking and decorating such a structure is a treasured holiday tradition. It all begins with a basic foundation of gingerbread sheets. Walls and roof are cut out around a paper pattern, then "glued" together with white royal icing that forms a very tight bond after it dries. Decorations, shutters, trees, and a chimney are created freehand. And you can actually eat it.

Gingerbread contruction has two schools of thought: a simple building, elaborately embellished, or an elaborate structure, simply finished. To get you started, we have designed a charming cottage that is neither fussy nor overly plain. It requires a minimum of pieces and is ready to customize with icing, embossing, and candy of every color. Enlarge the pattern pieces at right to cut out parts of the cottage, then follow the recipe and steps on the next three pages.

To make the gingerbread cottage, you will need the following ingredients and materials:

- One recipe Gingerbread Dough & Icing
- Peppermint candies, candy canes, sugar cubes, citrus-slice candies, gumdrops, and nonpareils
- Powdered Sugar
- Food Coloring
- Sugar ice cream cones
- Plastic or wooden board for a base
- Parchment paper or brown kraft paper
- Cardboard
- Pencil
- Baking sheet
- Mixing bowls, mixer, and small bowls
- Chef's knife
- Icing spatula
- Pastry bag and tips
- Hors d'oeuvre cutters

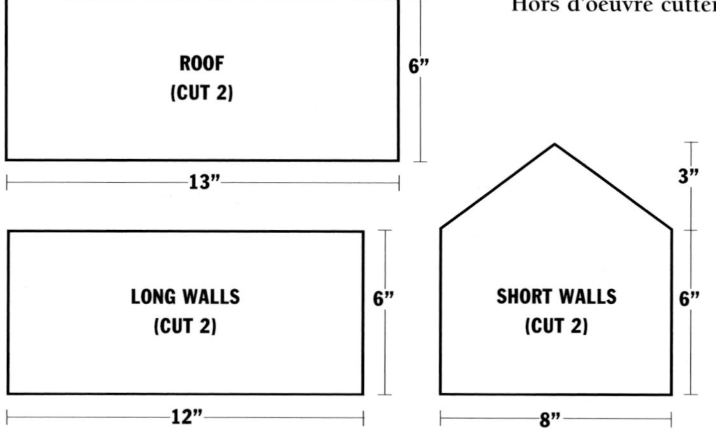

the moist dough will hold the paper pattern in place while you cut out the gingerbread pieces

use small holes created by a toothpick as guides when you draw the door and windows with icing

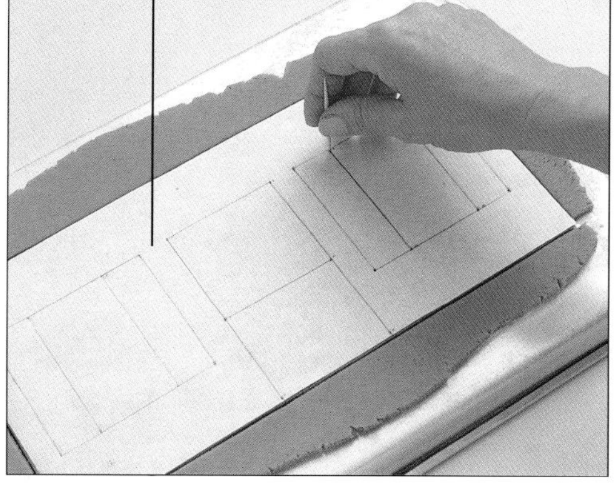

leave a margin of dough around the cutouts so they aren't hidden by the overhang of the roof

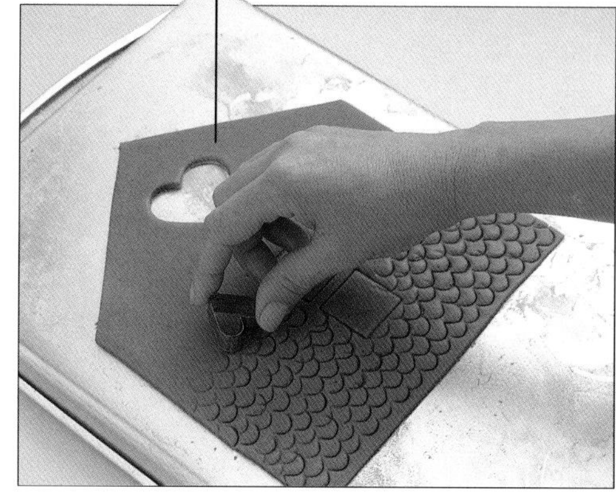

STEP 1 CUTTING COTTAGE SHAPES
Enlarge the patterns on page 52 to full size on parchment paper or brown kraft paper. Place 1 portion of dough at a time on the back of a 15x10x1-inch baking sheet or a large cookie sheet. Roll the dough slightly larger than the pattern piece and cut around the pattern with a knife. Slide excess dough away from main section; remove and wrap in plastic. Bake and repeat with each remaining portion of dough.

STEP 2 MARKING WINDOWS AND DOORS
Mark placement of windows and doors by poking a toothpick through the corners in the paper pattern. Remove the pattern. Score window and door outlines with a knife between corner marks.

STEP 3 MARKING TEXTURE IN WALLS
Texture walls with a small heart cutter, if desired. Use a 1½-inch heart cutter to cut the door and end-wall windows. Score roof pieces with an hors d'oeuvre cutter or knife.

GINGERBREAD DOUGH & ICING

Preparation Time: 4 hours
Baking Time: 10 to 12 minutes

INGREDIENTS

DOUGH

8	CUPS ALL-PURPOSE FLOUR
2	TEASPOONS GROUND GINGER
1-1/2	TEASPOONS GROUND CINNAMON
1	TEASPOON GROUND CLOVES
2-1/4	CUPS SHORTENING
2	CUPS GRANULATED SUGAR
2	EGGS
1	CUP LIGHT MOLASSES
2/3	CUP LIGHT CORN SYRUP

ICING

3	EGG WHITES, ROOM TEMPERATURE
1	16-OUNCE PACKAGE POWDERED SUGAR, SIFTED
1	TEASPOON VANILLA
1/2	TEASPOON CREAM OF TARTAR

■ For the dough, in a large mixing bowl, combine flour, ginger, cinnamon, and cloves; set aside.

■ In another bowl, beat shortening and sugar together till fluffy. Add eggs, molasses, and corn syrup. Beat till combined.

■ Add flour mixture gradually to shortening mixture. Beat well. If necessary, stir in the last 2 cups of the flour mixture, and knead dough till smooth. Divide dough into 6 equal portions. Cover.

■ Enlarge the pattern pieces for the house as directed in step 1. Cut out pattern pieces on parchment paper or kraft paper. Grease the back of a 15x10x1-inch baking pan or a large cookie sheet. Roll out one portion of the dough to a ¼-inch thickness on the greased pan. Place pattern piece on dough. Cut around piece with a knife. Remove excess dough. Mark windows, doors, and wall or roof texture as shown above.

■ Leave dough on the pan and bake in a preheated 375° oven for 10 to 12 minutes, or till edges are browned. Place pattern piece on the cookie piece and recut if necessary to make straight edges. Let cool 5 minutes on pan. Carefully transfer to a wire rack; cool completely. Repeat with remaining dough and patterns till all the house pieces are baked. Lightly knead and roll out the scraps; cut out rectangular shutters, if desired. Bake as directed.

■ Cool gingerbread pieces completely before beginning to assemble the cottage. If you allow the pieces to dry overnight, they will be even firmer and better for construction.

■ For the icing, in a large mixing bowl, combine egg whites, powdered sugar, vanilla, and cream of tartar. Beat with an electric mixer on high speed for 7 to 10 minutes, or till the mixture becomes very stiff. Use icing at once. Cover any icing in bowl at all times with plastic wrap to prevent drying.
Makes 6 portions dough and 3 cups icing

egg whites will beat to greater volume if they are at room temperature rather than cold

STEP 4 BEATING ICING TO STIFF PEAKS
Beat egg whites, powdered sugar, vanilla, and cream of tartar on high speed with an electric mixer until the icing is glossy and stands in stiff, straight peaks when the beaters are lifted.

to make shutters, reroll scraps and cut rectangles freehand; make heart-shaped perforations with a tiny cutter

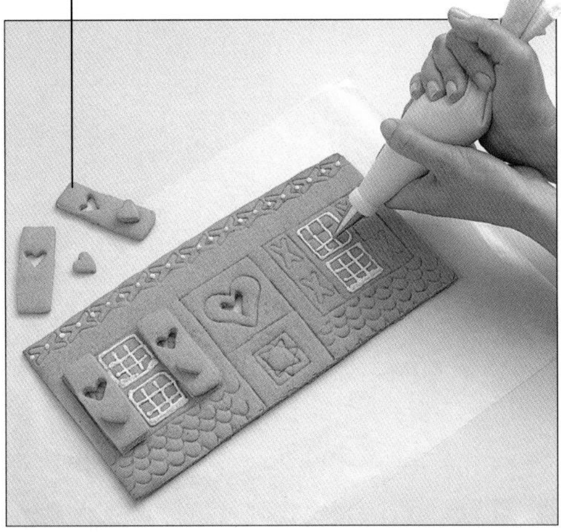

STEP 5 OUTLINING WITH ICING
Glue the shutters to the house with dabs of icing. Place icing in a pastry bag with a small, round writing tip. Use the icing to outline the windows, including the panes, and other architectural features.

STEP 6 DECORATING WITH CANDIES
Select candy that won't overwhelm the more subtle textures on the walls and roof. Study each side of the house before proceeding. Lay candy in place, but don't use icing "glue" just yet. If you are pleased with the effect, then attach the candy with the icing.

the icing will stay fluid because it is protected from air in the pastry bag

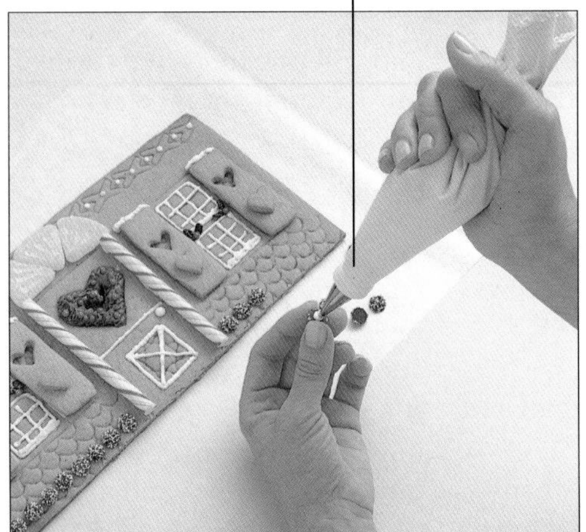

STEP 7 FINISHING WALLS
Continue to apply candy on all four walls until you are satisfied with the overall design. Check that each piece of candy is firmly attached. If any are loose when gently prodded, remove them. Pipe on more icing then put back in place.

STEP 8 ASSEMBLING HOUSE
Cut one short wall pattern out of cardboard for support; set aside. Mark a 12x8-inch baseline on a large plastic or wooden board. Pipe icing along the bottom and side edges of a short wall. Position on the baseline and support it with clay or food cans, if necessary.

For the long wall, pipe icing on the bottom edge and on the backside along the two short sides. Place long wall on the baseline next to the short wall. Pipe icing along the bottom and side edges of remaining short wall. Position on the baseline.

Pipe icing along the bottom and side edges of the cardboard support wall and place it inside the house, halfway between the short walls.

For the remaining long wall, pipe icing on the bottom edge and on the backside along the two short sides. Place the wall in position. Add extra icing as necessary to make strong corners. Let dry several hours or overnight before adding the roof.

For the roof, pipe a thick row of icing across the top edge of one long wall and along the adjoining top edges of each short wall, including the cardboard support wall. Position one roof section and hold until set. Repeat on the other side with the remaining roof section.

Reserve extra icing to build the chimney and create trees. If desired, prepare a second batch of icing to frost the yard.

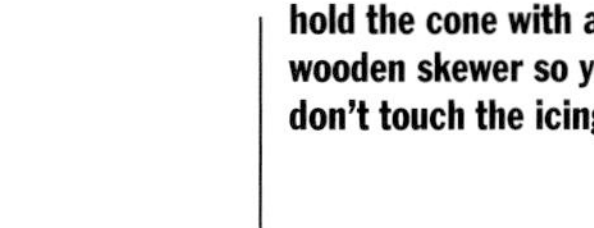

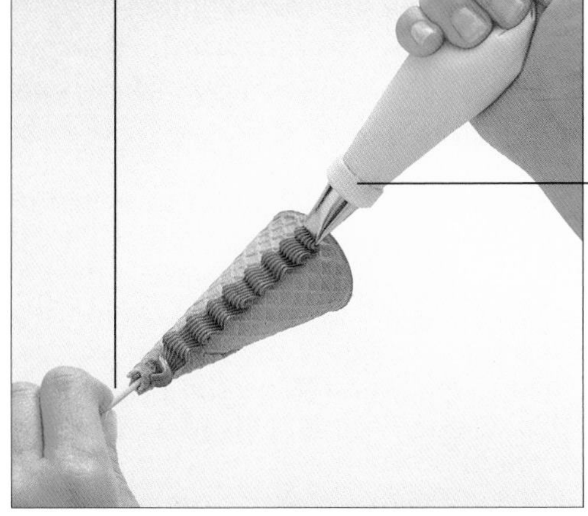

STEP 9 Building the Chimney

Stack sugar cubes using icing as mortar to make the chimney foundation. Pipe icing on the flat side of cocoa-dusted nuts or other candies that resemble large rocks. Begin at the chimney base and attach the nuts or candies to the sugar cubes. If your house is a formal style, line the nuts up; for a more casual style, apply them randomly as shown here.

STEP 10 Decorating the Trees

Tint extra icing with green food coloring. Pipe onto sugar ice cream cones with a leaf tip. Decorate as desired with candies, sprinkles, or a different color of icing to make a garland.

To finish the cottage, frost the surface of the base board with icing. Place trees in the icing and, if desired, create a path to the front door with peppermint candies. Pipe icing onto the roof edge to create icicles and dust the roof with powdered sugar. Sugar-cookie "kids" play in the front yard; to make them, use the recipe for Holiday Cookies on page 62.

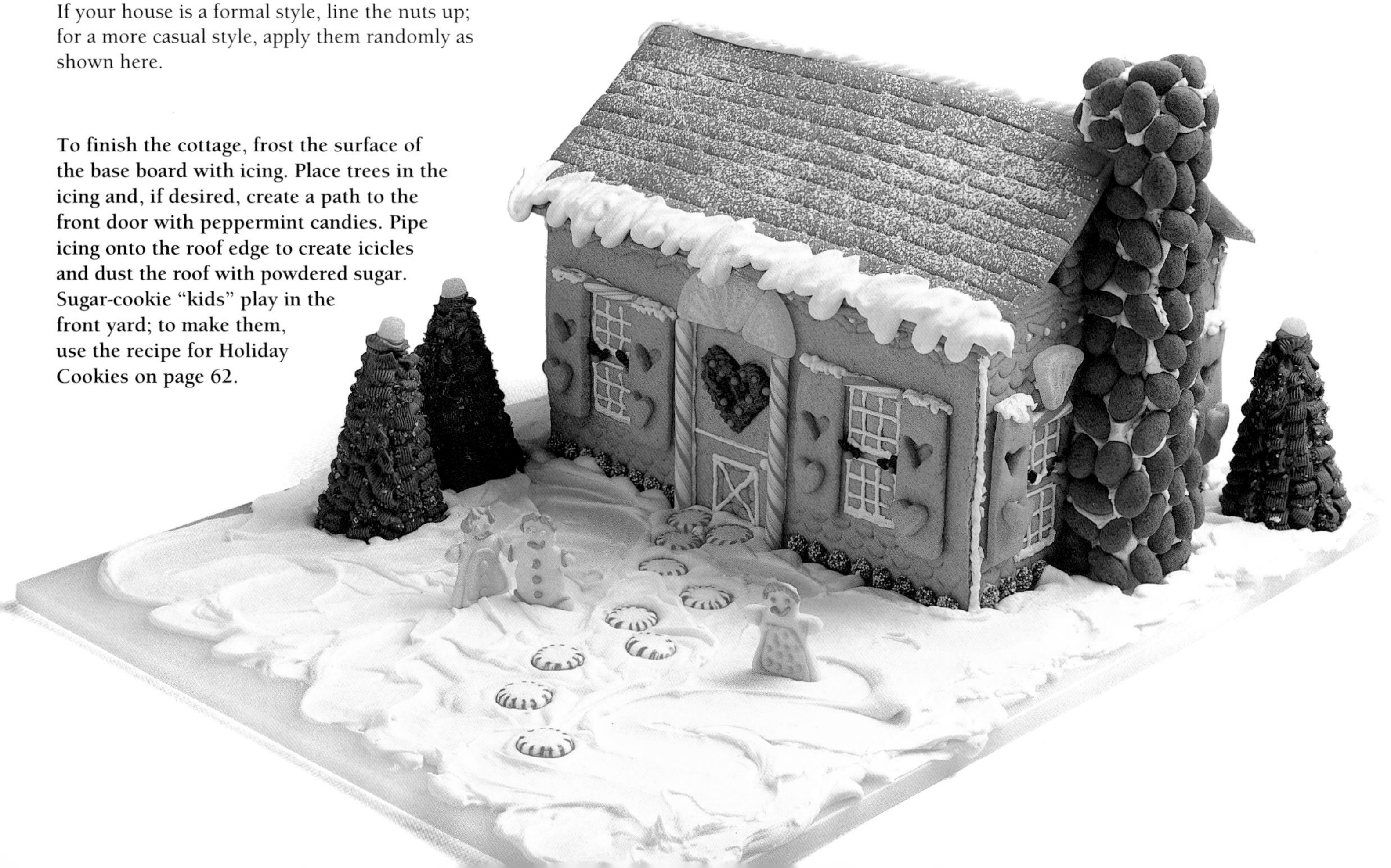

Linzer Sandwich Rings

Preparation Time: 40 minutes
Chilling Time: 1 hour
Baking Time: 7 to 9 minutes

INGREDIENTS

3/4	CUP BUTTER *OR* MARGARINE, SOFTENED
2/3	CUP PACKED BROWN SUGAR
1-1/2	TEASPOONS BAKING POWDER
1	TEASPOON FINELY SHREDDED LEMON PEEL
1	TEASPOON GROUND CINNAMON
1/4	TEASPOON GROUND ALLSPICE
1/4	TEASPOON SALT
2	EGG YOLKS
1	TEASPOON VANILLA
2	CUPS ALL-PURPOSE FLOUR
1	CUP GROUND WALNUTS *OR* ALMONDS
	SIFTED POWDERED SUGAR
1/4	CUP SEEDLESS RASPBERRY JAM

The combination of a ground almond pastry and raspberry jam is the basis for Linzertorte, a large version of these little cookies. Experiment with other types of jam and other nuts for the dough.

■ In a large mixing bowl beat the butter or margarine with an electric mixer on medium to high speed for 30 seconds. Add the brown sugar, baking powder, lemon peel, cinnamon, allspice, and salt and beat till combined. Beat in the egg yolks and vanilla. Beat in as much of the flour as you can with the mixer. Stir in any remaining flour and ground walnuts or almonds with a wooden spoon. Divide dough in half. Cover and chill for 1 hour, or till dough is easy to handle.

■ On a lightly floured surface, roll each half of dough to a ⅛-inch thickness. Using a 2- or 2½-inch scalloped round, star-, or heart-shaped cookie cutter, cut out dough. Place 1 inch apart on ungreased cookie sheets. Using a 1-inch cutter, cut out the centers of half of the unbaked cookies. Remove the centers and reroll dough to make more cookies.

■ Bake cookies in a preheated 375° oven for 7 to 9 minutes, or till edges are firm and bottoms are browned. Remove cookies and cool on a rack.

■ To assemble cookie sandwiches, sift powdered sugar over the tops of the cookies with cutouts in centers. Set aside. Spread about ½ teaspoon of the jam onto the bottom of each cookie without a cutout; top with a cutout cookie, powdered sugar–side up. (Store cookies unassembled, then assemble them up to several hours before serving.)

Makes about 36 cookies

Per cookie: 107 calories, 1 g protein, 12 g carbohydrate, 6 g total fat (3 g saturated), 22 mg cholesterol, 64 mg sodium, 43 mg potassium

STEPS AT A GLANCE	Page
GRINDING NUTS	18
MAKING COOKIE DOUGH	8
MAKING CUTOUT COOKIES	50
MAKING SANDWICH RINGS	56

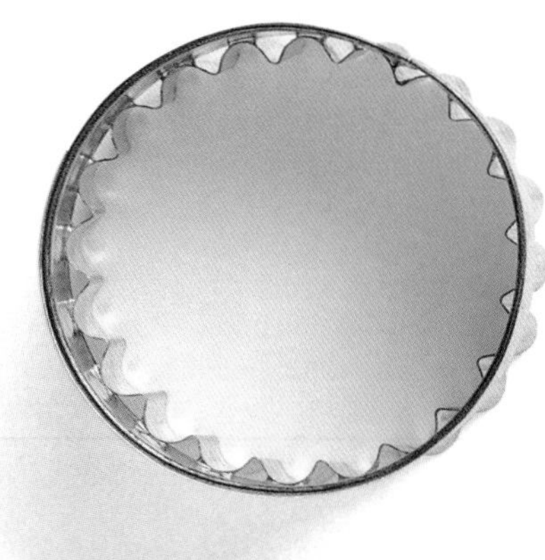

STEPS FOR MAKING SANDWICH RINGS

STEP 1 HOLLOWING CENTERS
Transfer the dough rounds to ungreased cookie sheets; arrange them 1 inch apart. Cut out the center of half of the unbaked cookies with a 1-inch cutter.

STEP 2 SPRINKLING SUGAR
Sift powdered sugar over the tops of the baked and cooled cutout cookies only. Use a powdered sugar sifter with a mesh cover, or a wire sieve.

STEP 3 ASSEMBLING RINGS
Spread a thin layer of raspberry preserves on the flat side of each bottom cookie. Set a cutout cookie over the preserves to make a "sandwich."

Decorative cutouts reveal a filling of raspberry preserves that glistens like stained glass. A sprinkling of powdered sugar creates a delicate frame.

Like real alpine snowflakes, no two of these iced, honey-and-spice-scented cookie stars are exactly alike.

Honey Snowflakes

INGREDIENTS

COOKIES

1/2	CUP BUTTER OR MARGARINE, SOFTENED
1/2	CUP PACKED BROWN SUGAR
1	TEASPOON BAKING POWDER
1/2	TEASPOON GROUND CARDAMOM
1	EGG
1/2	CUP HONEY
2	CUPS ALL-PURPOSE FLOUR
1	CUP WHOLE-WHEAT FLOUR

FROSTING

1/4	CUP BUTTER *OR* MARGARINE, SOFTENED
1/4	CUP ALL-PURPOSE FLOUR
2	TEASPOONS WATER

For this unusual recipe, the "frosting" bakes right along with the cookie. Don't worry about making too many; they store beautifully.

■ For cookies, in a mixing bowl beat the butter or margarine with an electric mixer on medium to high speed for 30 seconds. Add the brown sugar, baking powder, and cardamom; beat till combined. Beat in the egg and honey. Beat in as much of the all-purpose and whole-wheat flour as you can with a mixer. Stir in any remaining flour with a wooden spoon. Divide dough in half. Cover and chill for 3 hours, or till easy to handle.

■ For frosting, in a mixing bowl stir together the butter or margarine, flour, and water till smooth.

■ On a lightly floured surface, roll each half of dough to a 1/4-inch thickness. Using a 2- or 2 1/2-inch 6-pointed star or scalloped round cutter, cut dough into shapes. Place cookies 2 inches apart on ungreased cookie sheets. Pipe frosting on unbaked cookies with a decorating bag and writing tip.

■ Bake cookies in a preheated 375° oven for 7 to 9 minutes, or till edges are firm and bottoms are lightly browned. Remove cookies and cool on a rack.

Makes 4 to 5 dozen cookies

Per cookie: 75 calories, 1 g protein, 11 g carbohydrate, 3 g total fat (2 g saturated), 12 mg cholesterol, 36 mg sodium, 28 mg potassium

Preparation Time: 25 minutes
Chilling Time: 3 hours
Baking Time: 7 to 9 minutes

STEPS AT A GLANCE	Page
MAKING COOKIE DOUGH	8
MAKING CUTOUT COOKIES	50
DECORATING SNOWFLAKES	59

STEPS FOR DECORATING SNOWFLAKES

STEP 1 FILLING PASTRY BAG

Fit a pastry bag with a plain writing tip. Fold back the top of the bag to form a collar; slip one hand under the collar to steady the bag. With a rubber spatula, fill bag with frosting. Twist top of bag above frosting to close. Squeeze out a few inches of frosting to eliminate air bubbles.

STEP 2 PIPING FROSTING

Arrange the cookies 2 inches apart on ungreased cookie sheets. Pipe the frosting in delicate patterns on each cookie, squeezing the bag with steady, even pressure. Vary the pattern from cookie to cookie.

Raspberry Pinwheels

STEPS AT A GLANCE	Page
MAKING COOKIE DOUGH	8
MAKING CUTOUT COOKIES	50
MAKING PINWHEELS	60

Preparation Time: 30 minutes
Chilling Time: 3 hours
Baking Time: 8 to 10 minutes

INGREDIENTS

1/3	CUP BUTTER *OR* MARGARINE, SOFTENED
1	3-OUNCE PACKAGE CREAM CHEESE, SOFTENED
2/3	CUP GRANULATED SUGAR
1	TEASPOON BAKING POWDER
1	EGG
1	TEASPOON VANILLA
2	CUPS ALL-PURPOSE FLOUR
1/3	CUP SEEDLESS RED RASPBERRY, STRAWBERRY, *OR* APRICOT PRESERVES
1/4	CUP FINELY CHOPPED PISTACHIO NUTS *OR* ALMONDS

This cookie dough is sturdy enough to withstand cutting and shaping, yet it remains rich and tasty. Serve these beauties at your next party.

■ In a mixing bowl beat the butter or margarine and cream cheese with an electric mixer on medium to high speed for 30 seconds. Add the sugar and baking powder; beat till combined. Beat in the egg and vanilla. Beat in as much of the flour as you can with a mixer. Stir in any remaining flour with a wooden spoon. Divide dough in half. Cover and chill for about 3 hours, or till the dough is easy to handle.

■ On a lightly floured surface, roll each half of the dough to a 10-inch square. Using a pastry wheel or sharp knife, cut each square into sixteen 2½-inch squares. Place ½ inch apart on ungreased cookie sheets. Use a knife to cut 1-inch slits from each corner to center. Drop ½ teaspoon of the preserves in each center. Fold every other tip to the center to form a pinwheel. Sprinkle chopped nuts in the center and press firmly to seal.

■ Bake in a preheated 350° oven for 8 to 10 minutes, or till edges are firm and lightly browned. Cool on cookie sheets for 1 minute. Remove cookies and cool on a rack.

Makes about 32 cookies

Per cookie: 86 calories, 1 g protein, 12 g carbohydrate, 4 g total fat (2 g saturated), 15 mg cholesterol, 33 mg sodium, 27 mg potassium

STEPS FOR MAKING PINWHEELS

STEP 1 CUTTING SQUARES
On a lightly floured surface, roll out each half of chilled dough to a 10-inch square (trim to exact dimensions). With a plain or fluted pastry wheel, cut each into sixteen 2½-inch squares.

STEP 2 CUTTING SLITS
Transfer the squares to ungreased baking sheets. Use a sharp knife to cut 1-inch slits from each corner to the center. If needed, dip the knife blade in flour to keep the dough from sticking to it.

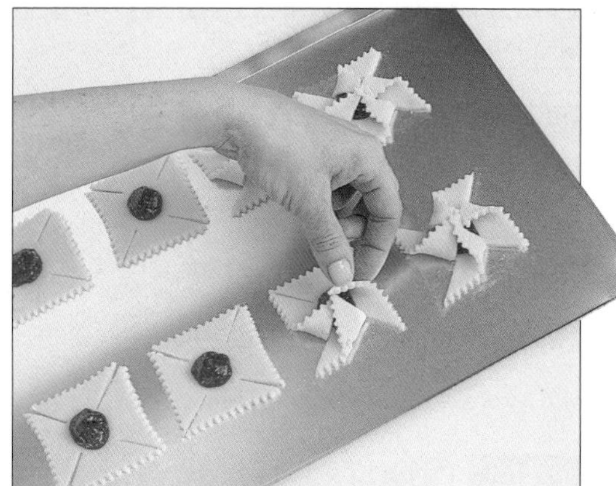

STEP 3 SHAPING COOKIES
Place ½ teaspoon of the preserves in the center of each cookie. Fold over every other tip to the center to form the pinwheel. The dough will stick to the preserves. Sprinkle with chopped nuts.

Sophisticated cookie pinwheels seem to be in motion even when resting on a serving plate. Glossy fruit preserves and a delicate sprinkle of chopped nuts dot the center of each.

Holiday Cookies

Preparation Time: 30 minutes
Chilling Time: 3 hours
Baking Time: 7 to 8 minutes

INGREDIENTS

COOKIES	
1/3	CUP SHORTENING
1/3	CUP BUTTER *OR* MARGARINE, SOFTENED
3/4	CUP GRANULATED SUGAR
1	TEASPOON BAKING POWDER
1/4	TEASPOON SALT
1	EGG
1	TABLESPOON MILK
1	TEASPOON VANILLA
2	CUPS ALL-PURPOSE FLOUR

ICING	
1	CUP SIFTED POWDERED SUGAR
1/4	TEASPOON VANILLA
1	TABLESPOON MILK
	FEW DROPS FOOD COLORING (OPTIONAL)

Children will have a great time helping decorate the myriad shapes that may be cut from this basic cookie dough.

■ For cookies, in a large mixing bowl beat the shortening and butter or margarine with an electric mixer on medium to high speed for 30 seconds. Add the sugar, baking powder, and salt; beat till combined. Beat in the egg, milk and vanilla. Beat in as much of the flour as you can with a mixer. Stir in any remaining flour with a wooden spoon. Divide dough in half. Cover and chill for 3 hours, or till dough is easy to handle.

■ On a lightly floured surface, roll each half of the dough to a ⅛-inch thickness. Using 2- or 2½-inch cutters, cut dough into desired holiday shapes, such as hearts, shamrocks, eggs, rabbits, flags, turkeys, pumpkins, or trees. Place 1 inch apart on ungreased cookie sheets.

■ Bake in a preheated 375° oven for 7 to 8 minutes, or till edges are firm and bottoms are lightly browned. Remove cookies and cool on a rack.

■ Meanwhile, for icing, in a small mixing bowl stir together powdered sugar, vanilla, and enough of the milk to make an icing of piping consistency. If desired, stir in food coloring. Use a pastry bag and writing tip to decorate cookies with icing.

Makes 36 to 48 cookies

Per cookie: 95 calories, 1 g protein, 15 g carbohydrate, 4 g total fat (2 g saturated), 11 mg cholesterol, 39 mg sodium, 12 mg potassium

Eat your way through the holidays by making buttery sugar-cookie cutouts for every festive occasion. Tinted icing gives them personality.

STEPS AT A GLANCE	Page
MAKING COOKIE DOUGH	8
MAKING CUTOUT COOKIES	50

Chocolate-Cherry Parson's Hats

You can use green maraschino cherries, pieces of other kinds of candied fruit, or different flavors of preserves to make infinite variations on this recipe.

■ In a mixing bowl beat the butter or margarine with an electric mixer on medium to high speed for 30 seconds. Add the sugar, cocoa powder, and baking powder; beat till combined. Beat in the egg and almond extract. Beat in as much of the flour as you can with the mixer. Stir in any remaining flour with a wooden spoon. Cover and chill for 3 hours, or till dough is easy to handle.

■ On a lightly floured surface, roll dough to a ¼-inch thickness. Using a 2½-inch round cutter, cut dough into rounds. Place a maraschino cherry or 1 teaspoon of the cherry preserves onto the center of each round.

■ To form each tricornered hat, lift up 3 edges of each dough round. Fold the edges toward, but not over, the filling. Then pinch the 3 outer points together. Place cookies 2 inches apart on ungreased cookie sheets.

■ Bake in a preheated 350° oven for 10 to 12 minutes, or till edges are firm. Remove cookies and cool on a rack.

■ In a small, heavy saucepan, melt candy coating and shortening over low heat; drizzle over cookies.

Makes about 30 cookies

Per cookie: 196 calories, 21 g protein, 18 g carbohydrate, 4 g fat (1 g saturated), 69 mg cholesterol, 311 mg sodium, 286 mg potassium

INGREDIENTS

3/4	CUP BUTTER *OR* MARGARINE, SOFTENED
3/4	CUP GRANULATED SUGAR
1/3	CUP UNSWEETENED COCOA POWDER
1/2	TEASPOON BAKING POWDER
1	EGG
1/4	TEASPOON ALMOND EXTRACT
1-3/4	CUPS ALL-PURPOSE FLOUR
30	MARASCHINO CHERRIES, *OR* 1/2 CUP CHERRY PRESERVES
1-1/2	OUNCES WHITE BAKING BAR
1	TEASPOON SHORTENING

Preparation Time: 25 minutes
Chilling Time: 3 hours
Baking Time: 10 to 12 minutes

STEPS AT A GLANCE	Page
MAKING COOKIE DOUGH	8
MAKING CUTOUT COOKIES	50
DRIZZLING ICING OR CHOCOLATE	11

A sweet maraschino cherry peeks out of each icing-drizzled chocolate tricorn.

Molasses & Ginger Stars

INGREDIENTS

DOUGH

1	CUP BUTTER *OR* MARGARINE, SOFTENED
2/3	CUP PACKED BROWN SUGAR
1	TABLESPOON VERY FINELY CHOPPED CRYSTALLIZED GINGER *OR* 1 TEASPOON GROUND GINGER
1/2	TEASPOON BAKING SODA
1/2	CUP MOLASSES
1/3	CUP MILK
3-1/2	CUPS ALL-PURPOSE FLOUR

ICING

3	CUPS SIFTED POWDERED SUGAR
2	TO 3 TABLESPOONS MILK
	FINELY CHOPPED CRYSTALLIZED GINGER (OPTIONAL)

Preparation Time: 25 minutes
Chilling Time: 3 hours
Baking Time: 7 to 9 minutes

STEPS AT A GLANCE	Page
MAKING COOKIE DOUGH	8
MAKING CUTOUT COOKIES	50
DRIZZLING ICING OR CHOCOLATE	11

These spicy, crisp cookies are a perfect autumn sweet. Look for crystallized (candied) ginger among the other spices at your supermarket, or at a gourmet specialty store.

■ For dough, in a large mixing bowl beat butter or margarine with an electric mixer on medium to high speed for 30 seconds. Add the brown sugar, crystallized or ground ginger, and baking soda; beat till combined. Beat in molasses and milk. Beat in as much of the flour as you can with a mixer. Stir in any remaining flour with a wooden spoon. Divide dough in half. Cover and chill for 3 hours, or till easy to handle.

■ On a lightly floured surface, roll each half of dough to a ¼-inch thickness. Using a 2-inch star cutter, cut dough into star shapes. Place cookies 1 inch apart on greased cookie sheets.

■ Bake in a preheated 375° oven for about 7 to 9 minutes, or till edges are firm. Remove cookies and cool on a rack.

■ Meanwhile, for icing, in a medium mixing bowl stir together the powdered sugar and enough of the milk to make an icing of drizzling consistency. Drizzle icing over cookies. If desired, decorate with additional crystallized ginger.

Makes about 60 cookies

Per cookie: 89 calories, 1 g protein, 15 g carbohydrate, 3 g total fat (2 g saturated), 8 mg cholesterol, 45 mg sodium, 45 mg potassium

Little stars flavored with molasses and crystallized ginger will remind you of crisp gingerbread, a classic holiday cookie.

Meringue-topped Lemon Thins

Sophisticated meringue and slivered almonds top delicate, meltingly tender lemon crescents.

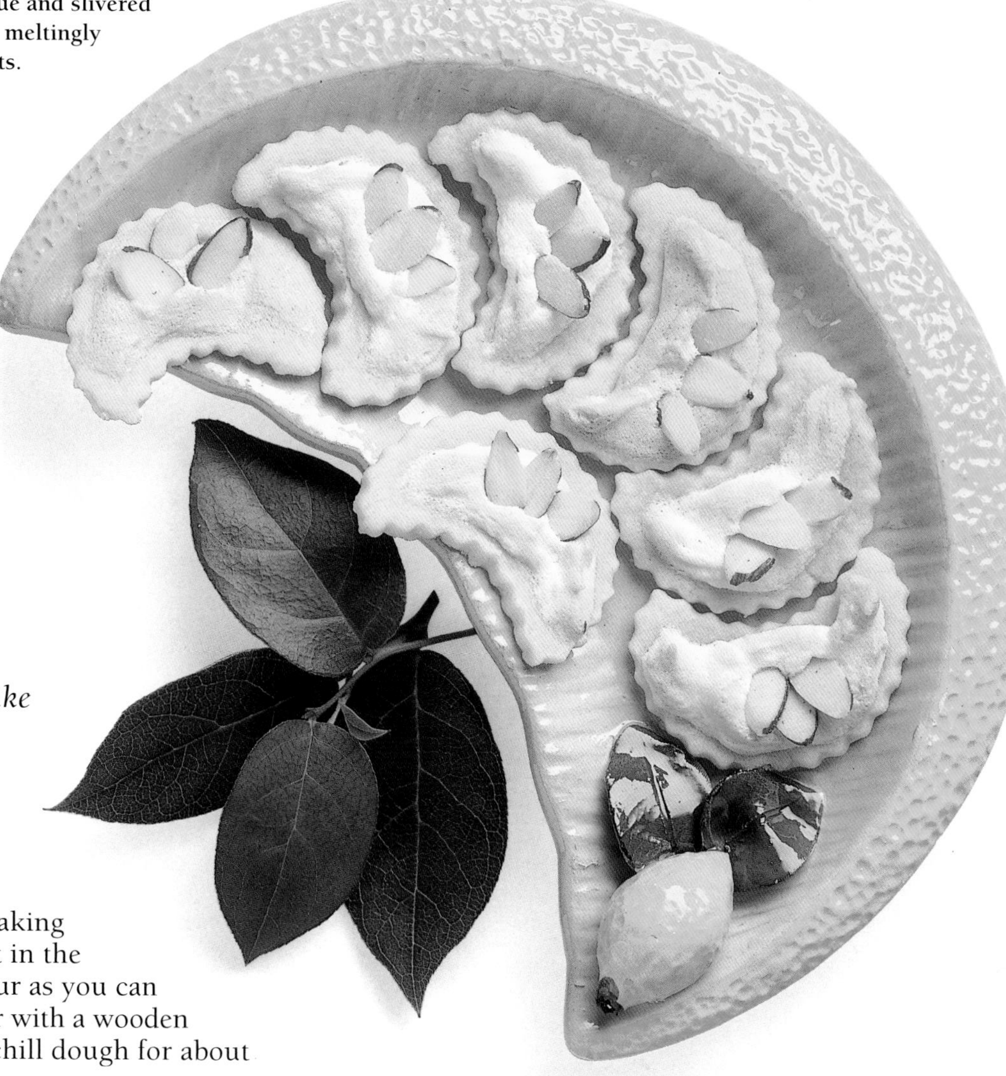

Preparation Time: 30 minutes
Chilling Time: 3 hours
Baking Time: 11 minutes

INGREDIENTS

1	CUP BUTTER *OR* MARGARINE, SOFTENED
1/2	CUP GRANULATED SUGAR
1	TABLESPOON FINELY SHREDDED LEMON PEEL
1/4	TEASPOON BAKING POWDER
1/4	TEASPOON SALT
1/4	TEASPOON LEMON EXTRACT
2	CUPS ALL-PURPOSE FLOUR
2	EGG WHITES
2/3	CUP SUGAR
1/2	CUP SLICED ALMONDS

The meringue on these dainty waferlike cookies bakes into a wonderfully chewy topping.

■ In a large mixing bowl beat the butter or margarine with an electric mixer on medium to high speed for 30 seconds. Add ½ cup sugar, lemon peel, baking powder, and salt; beat till combined. Beat in the lemon extract. Beat in as much of the flour as you can with the mixer. Stir in any remaining flour with a wooden spoon. Divide dough in half. Cover and chill dough for about 3 hours, or till easy to handle.

■ On a lightly floured surface, roll each half of dough to a ¼-inch thickness. Cut into desired shapes using 2- or 2½-inch cookie cutters. Place 1 inch apart on ungreased cookie sheets.

■ In another mixing bowl beat the egg whites with an electric mixer till soft peaks form. Gradually beat in the ⅔ cup sugar till stiff peaks form. Spread 1 rounded teaspoon over each cookie; sprinkle a few sliced almonds over each cookie. (Chill egg white mixture between batches.)

■ Bake in a preheated 350° oven for about 11 minutes, or till meringue is lightly browned. Remove cookies and cool on a rack.

Makes about 42 cookies

Per cookie: 90 calories, 1 g protein, 10 g carbohydrate, 5 g total fat (3 g saturated), 12 mg cholesterol, 68 mg sodium, 22 mg potassium

STEPS AT A GLANCE	Page
MAKING COOKIE DOUGH	8
MAKING CUTOUT COOKIES	50
MAKING MERINGUE	11

Fruity Foldovers

Soft, fruit-filled cookies are loved by both children and adults. Here's an easy version that will please the whole family. The cookies store well in an airtight container at room temperature or in the freezer.

■ In a mixing bowl beat butter or margarine with an electric mixer on medium to high speed for 30 seconds. Add brown sugar, baking soda, coriander, and salt; beat till combined. Beat in the egg, honey, and vanilla. Beat in as much of the flour as you can with a mixer. Stir in any remaining flour with a wooden spoon. Divide dough in half. Cover and chill for 3 hours, or till dough is easy to handle.

■ Meanwhile, in a small saucepan heat apple or currant jelly till melted. Remove from heat. Stir in the dried fruit and pecans or walnuts.

■ On a lightly floured surface roll each half of the dough to a ⅛-inch thickness. Using a 2½-inch round cookie cutter, cut into rounds. Place cookies ½ inch apart on ungreased cookie sheets.

■ Spoon 1 teaspoon of the dried fruit mixture onto the center of each round. Fold half of the round over filling, creating a half-moon shape. Seal cut edges of each round with the tines of a fork.

■ Bake in a preheated 375° oven for 7 to 9 minutes, or till bottoms are lightly browned. Remove cookies and cool on a rack. Sprinkle with powdered sugar.

Makes about 50 cookies

Per cookie: 72 calories, 1 g protein, 12 g carbohydrate, 3 g total fat (1 g saturated), 9 mg cholesterol, 44 mg sodium, 38 mg potassium

STEPS AT A GLANCE	Page
SNIPPING FRUIT	21
MAKING COOKIE DOUGH	8
MAKING CUTOUT COOKIES	50

Preparation Time: 40 minutes
Chilling Time: 3 hours
Baking Time: 7 to 9 minutes

INGREDIENTS

1/2	CUP BUTTER *OR* MARGARINE, SOFTENED
1/4	CUP PACKED BROWN SUGAR
1/2	TEASPOON BAKING SODA
1/2	TEASPOON GROUND CORIANDER
1/4	TEASPOON SALT
1	EGG
1/2	CUP HONEY
1	TEASPOON VANILLA
2-1/2	CUPS ALL-PURPOSE FLOUR
1/3	CUP APPLE *OR* CURRANT JELLY
1	CUP SNIPPED MIXED DRIED FRUITS (SUCH AS APRICOTS, APPLES, PEACHES, PRUNES, *OR* DATES, *OR* RAISINS)
1/2	CUP FINELY CHOPPED PECANS *OR* WALNUTS
	SIFTED POWDERED SUGAR

Sugar-dusted cookie turnovers filled with a harvest of dried fruits and nuts resemble miniature hand-held pies.

Sliced Cookies

Steps for Making Sliced Cookies

Basic Tools for Making Sliced Cookies

For sliced cookies, it's best to chill the log of dough in a tall glass so it won't flatten, then when firm, cut it into rounds with a sharp knife and bake on a cookie sheet. Use a spatula to transfer the finished cookies to a wire cooling rack.

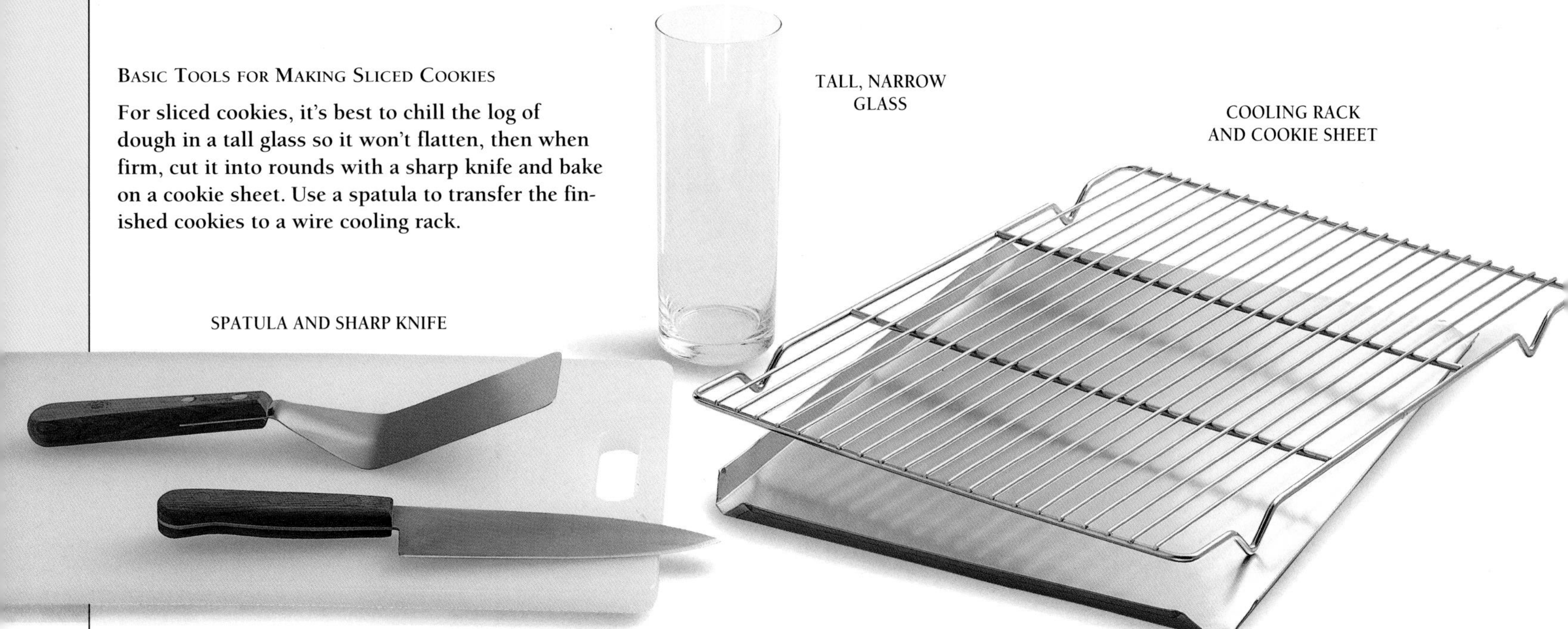

TALL, NARROW GLASS

COOLING RACK AND COOKIE SHEET

SPATULA AND SHARP KNIFE

CUTTING BOARD

SLICED COOKIES are the ultimate in convenience. Once made, the rich dough can wait in the refrigerator for up to 1 week until you need it. In fact, chilling is a must because the dough is too soft to cut initially, much like the mixture used for cutout cookies. The two doughs are similar in their early stages — both have similar consistencies and are refrigerated — but differ in how they are shaped. While cutouts are punched out of a rolled dough sheet, sliced cookies are cut from a solid dough log. To add texture and flavor, some doughs are rolled in chopped nuts, like Chocolate-Pistachio Sandwich Cookies (page 73), or tinted with chocolate, sliced, and reassembled into two-color checkerboards like those on page 70 or stacked into stripes like the Chocolate-Peppermint Slices on page 76. A nicely rounded shape is an important part of the visual appeal of these cookies. If the dough flattens as you slice it, roll it back into a log and chill it again for about 5 to 10 minutes.

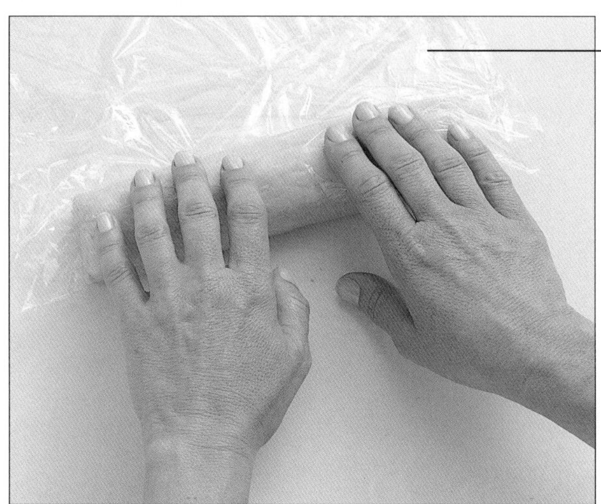

STEP 1 **Shaping Dough**

Divide the dough in half. Place each half on a sheet of plastic wrap large enough to fully enclose it. Roll the dough into a log inside the wrap. Seal the ends airtight.

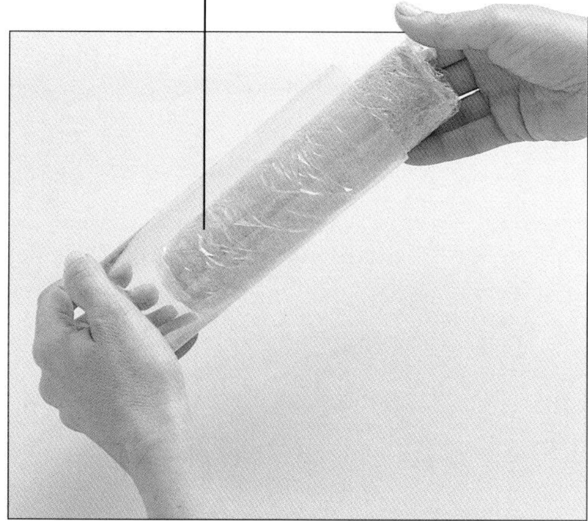

STEP 2 Storing Log of Dough

To keep the log nicely rounded, chill it inside a tall, narrow glass (if the log is longer than your glass, cut it into several portions and store it in several glasses). Alternatively, just chill the dough wrapped in plastic.

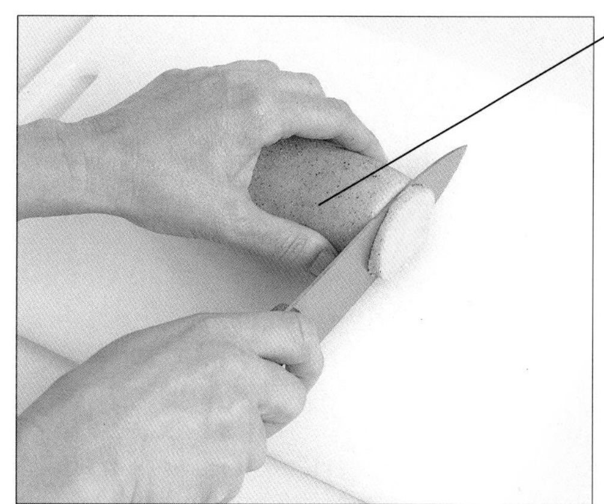

STEP 3 Slicing Cookies

Unwrap the chilled log of dough. Cut it into ¼-inch-thick slices with a sharp knife. Always use a knife with a thin, sharp blade and slice with a back-and-forth sawing motion, not a downward swipe.

STEP 4 Testing for Doneness

Bake in a preheated 375° oven until the edges are firm and the bottoms are lightly browned, about 8 to 10 minutes, or as the recipe directs. Remove from the cookie sheet to a wire rack to cool completely.

Although they look plain, these simple sliced cookies are full of flavor. Sugar-topped Rum & Spice Cookies are on page 74.

Chocolate & Vanilla Checkerboards

Preparation Time: 45 minutes
Chilling Time: 2 hours
Baking Time: 8 to 10 minutes

INGREDIENTS

1	CUP BUTTER *OR* MARGARINE, SOFTENED
1/2	CUP GRANULATED SUGAR
1/2	CUP PACKED BROWN SUGAR
1-1/2	TEASPOONS BAKING POWDER
1	EGG
2	TEASPOONS VANILLA
3-1/4	CUPS ALL-PURPOSE FLOUR
2	OUNCES UNSWEETENED CHOCOLATE, MELTED

So easy, yet so dramatic. And you don't really need to tell anyone how simple these checkerboard cookies are to make. If pressed for time, make and assemble the spliced logs, then chill until the next day when all you need to do is to slice and bake them.

■ In a large mixing bowl beat the butter or margarine with an electric mixer on medium to high speed for 30 seconds. Add the granulated sugar, brown sugar, and baking powder; beat till combined. Beat in the egg and vanilla. Beat in as much of the flour as you can with the mixer. Stir in any remaining flour with a wooden spoon. Divide dough in half.

■ Knead melted chocolate into half of dough till combined. Shape plain and chocolate halves of dough into 8-inch logs. Wrap each in waxed paper or plastic wrap. Chill for 2 hours, or till firm. Cut each chilled log lengthwise into quarters; reassemble logs, alternating chocolate and vanilla quarters. Wrap and refrigerate for 15 to 30 minutes, or till well chilled.

■ Cut dough into ¼-inch-thick slices. Place 2 inches apart on ungreased cookie sheets. Bake in a preheated 375° oven for 8 to 10 minutes, or till edges are firm and bottoms are lightly browned. Remove cookies and cool on a rack.

Makes about 64 cookies

Per cookie: 65 calories, 1 g protein, 8 g carbohydrate, 3 g total fat (2 g saturated), 11 mg cholesterol, 36 mg sodium, 22 mg potassium

STEPS AT A GLANCE	Page
MELTING CHOCOLATE	10
MAKING COOKIE DOUGH	8
MAKING CHECKERBOARD COOKIES	70

STEPS FOR MAKING CHECKERBOARD COOKIES

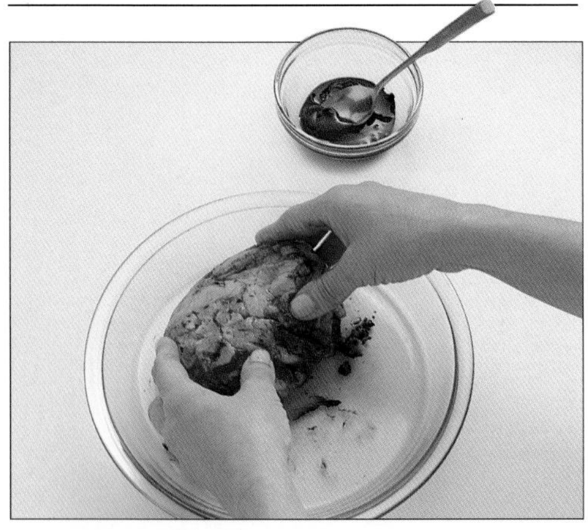

STEP 1 ADDING CHOCOLATE
Divide the dough into 2 equal pieces. Knead the melted chocolate into 1 piece of dough until completely blended without any streaks remaining.

STEP 2 CUTTING DOUGH
Be sure the dough is thoroughly chilled. Cut each chocolate and vanilla log into quarters with a knife that is very sharp and has a long, thin blade.

STEP 3 REASSEMBLING LOGS
Press together 1 chocolate piece and 1 vanilla piece to form a half moon. Set another chocolate piece on top of the vanilla. Insert a vanilla piece next to it. You should now have a whole log with alternating chocolate and vanilla quarters. Wrap tightly and chill.

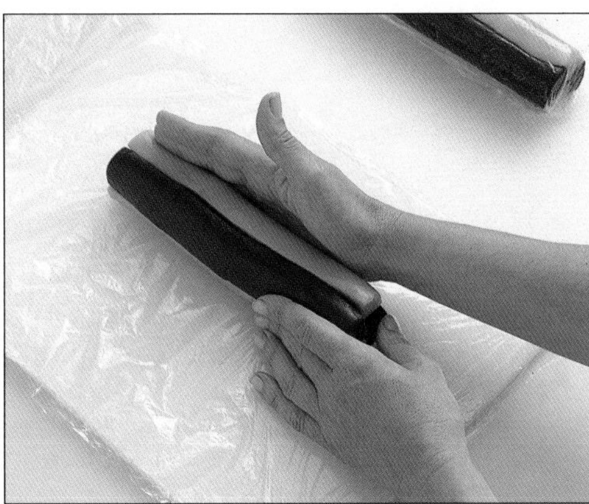

Simple two-tone checkerboards are very impressive. They look marvelous and taste as good as they look.

Pale green pistachio nuts form a halo of color and texture on the edges of chocolate sandwiches filled with an enticing milk-chocolate butter cream.

Chocolate-Pistachio Sandwich Cookies

INGREDIENTS

COOKIES

1	CUP BUTTER *OR* MARGARINE, SOFTENED
1	CUP GRANULATED SUGAR
1/2	CUP PACKED BROWN SUGAR
1/3	CUP UNSWEETENED COCOA POWDER
1	TEASPOON BAKING POWDER
1/4	TEASPOON GROUND NUTMEG
1	EGG
1-1/2	TEASPOONS VANILLA
2	CUPS ALL-PURPOSE FLOUR
2/3	CUP GROUND PISTACHIOS, ALMONDS, *OR* PECANS

FILLING

3	TABLESPOONS BUTTER *OR* MARGARINE, SOFTENED
1/4	CUP UNSWEETENED COCOA POWDER
2	CUPS SIFTED POWDERED SUGAR
2	TABLESPOONS MILK
3/4	TEASPOON VANILLA
	MILK

Some specialty or natural foods stores carry shelled pistachios in bulk, which makes cooking with them cheaper and easier on the fingers than having to shell them at home.

■ For cookies, in a large mixing bowl beat the butter or margarine with an electric mixer on medium to high speed for 30 seconds. Add the granulated sugar, brown sugar, cocoa powder, baking powder, and nutmeg; beat till combined. Beat in the egg and vanilla. Beat in as much of the flour as you can with the mixer. Stir in any remaining flour with a wooden spoon. Divide dough in half. Cover and chill for 30 minutes, or till dough can be shaped into rolls. Shape dough into two 8-inch rolls. Roll in ground pistachios, almonds, or pecans to coat. Wrap in waxed paper or plastic wrap. Chill dough for 2 hours, or till firm.

■ For filling, in a bowl beat butter or margarine till fluffy. Beat in cocoa powder. Gradually add 1 cup of the powdered sugar, beating well. Slowly beat in the milk and vanilla. Gradually beat in the remaining powdered sugar. Beat in additional milk, if needed, to make a mixture of spreading consistency.

■ Cut dough into ¼-inch-thick slices. Place 2 inches apart on ungreased cookie sheets. Bake in a preheated 375° oven for 8 to 10 minutes, or till edges are firm. Remove cookies and cool on a rack.

■ Spread 1 to 2 teaspoons of the filling over the bottoms of half the cookies; top with remaining cookies, bottom sides down.
Makes about 32 cookies

Per cookie: 174 calories, 2 g protein, 23 g carbohydrate, 9 g total fat (4 g saturated), 25 mg cholesterol, 83 mg sodium, 57 mg potassium

Preparation Time: 45 minutes
Chilling Time: 2 hours
Baking Time: 8 to 10 minutes

STEPS AT A GLANCE	Page
GRINDING NUTS	18
MAKING COOKIE DOUGH	8
MAKING SANDWICH COOKIES	73

STEPS FOR MAKING SANDWICH COOKIES

STEP 1 COATING WITH NUTS
Arrange the ground nuts in an 8-inch square on a sheet of waxed paper. Gently roll a log of chocolate cookie dough across the nuts.

STEP 2 MAKING FILLING
Gradually beat the powdered sugar and milk in small amounts into the cocoa-margarine mixture, alternating sugar and milk until the mixture is creamy and ready to spread.

Rum & Spice Cookies

Rum-flavored spice cookies glitter with a topping of sugar crystals and allspice.

Preparation Time: 30 minutes
Chilling Time: 2 to 3 hours
Baking Time: 8 to 10 minutes

INGREDIENTS

3/4	CUP BUTTER *OR* MARGARINE, SOFTENED
1	CUP GRANULATED SUGAR
1	TEASPOON BAKING POWDER
1/2	TEASPOON BAKING SODA
1/2	TEASPOON GROUND ALLSPICE
1	EGG
1/4	CUP HONEY
3	TABLESPOONS RUM
2-2/3	CUPS ALL-PURPOSE FLOUR
1/3	CUP GRANULATED SUGAR
3/4	TEASPOON GROUND ALLSPICE

Try brandy in place of the rum or, for a nonalcoholic version, substitute 3 tablespoons of water and ½ teaspoon rum extract for the rum.

■ In a large mixing bowl beat the butter or margarine with an electric mixer on medium to high speed for 30 seconds. Add 1 cup sugar, baking powder, baking soda, and ½ teaspoon allspice; beat till combined. Beat in the egg, honey, and rum. Beat in as much of the flour as you can with the mixer. Stir in any remaining flour with a wooden spoon. Divide dough in half. If necessary, cover and chill for 1 hour, or till dough can be shaped into rolls.

■ In a 9-inch pie plate, stir together ⅓ cup sugar and ¾ teaspoon allspice. Shape each half of dough into an 8-inch roll; roll each in the sugar-allspice mixture to coat. Wrap in waxed paper or plastic wrap. Chill for 2 hours, or till firm. Cover and reserve remaining sugar and spice mixture.

■ Cut the chilled dough into ¼-inch-thick slices. Place slices about 2 inches apart on lightly greased cookie sheets. Sprinkle with reserved sugar-allspice mixture. Bake in a preheated 375° oven for 8 to 10 minutes, or till edges are firm and bottoms are lightly browned. Remove cookies and cool on a rack.

Makes about 64 cookies

Per cookie: 58 calories, 1 g protein, 9 g carbohydrate, 2 g total fat (1 g saturated), 9 mg cholesterol, 36 mg sodium, 9 mg potassium

STEPS AT A GLANCE	Page
MAKING COOKIE DOUGH	8
MAKING SLICED COOKIES	68

Mocha Tea Cookies

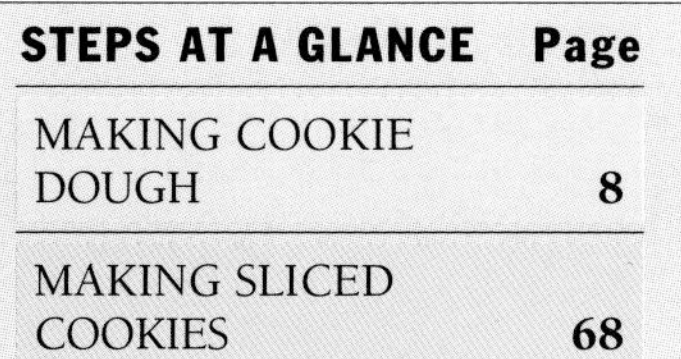

STEPS AT A GLANCE	Page
MAKING COOKIE DOUGH	8
MAKING SLICED COOKIES	68

Preparation Time: 25 minutes
Chilling Time: 2 hours
Baking Time: 8 to 10 minutes

INGREDIENTS

COOKIES

3/4	CUP BUTTER *OR* MARGARINE, SOFTENED
1/3	CUP PACKED BROWN SUGAR
1/3	CUP UNSWEETENED COCOA POWDER
1	TEASPOON INSTANT ESPRESSO COFFEE POWDER
1	TEASPOON VANILLA
1/8	TEASPOON SALT
1-1/2	CUPS ALL-PURPOSE FLOUR

FROSTING

3	TABLESPOONS BUTTER *OR* MARGARINE
2-1/4	CUPS SIFTED POWDERED SUGAR
1	TEASPOON VANILLA
1	TO 2 TABLESPOONS MILK

The word mocha, *which we use to mean a chocolate-coffee combination, comes from the name of a port in Yemen where coffee trees were first cultivated. Here powdered cocoa provides the chocolate flavor and instant espresso powder the coffee.*

■ For cookies, in a large mixing bowl beat butter or margarine with an electric mixer on medium to high speed for 30 seconds. Add the brown sugar, cocoa powder, espresso powder, vanilla, and salt; beat till combined. Beat in as much of the flour as you can with the mixer. Stir in any remaining flour with a wooden spoon. Shape dough into one 10-inch roll. Wrap in waxed paper or plastic wrap. Chill dough for 2 hours, or till firm.

■ Cut dough into ¼-inch-thick slices. Place about 2 inches apart on lightly greased cookie sheets. Bake in a preheated 375° oven for 8 to 10 minutes, or till edges are firm and bottoms are lightly browned. Remove cookies and cool on a rack.

■ Meanwhile, for frosting, in a medium saucepan melt butter or margarine and stir over medium heat till butter browns. Remove from heat; stir in powdered sugar, vanilla, and enough of the milk to make a frosting of spreading consistency. If frosting becomes too stiff, add hot water, a few drops at a time, and stir till smooth.

Makes about 36 cookies

Per cookie: 94 calories, 1 g protein, 13 g carbohydrate, 5 g total fat (2 g saturated), 10 mg cholesterol, 60 mg sodium, 19 mg potassium

A crown of silken white frosting tops these mocha-flavored cookie slices.

Chocolate-Peppermint Slices

If everyone is tired of plain old sugar cookies, make this delightful variation instead. You can make the peppermint dough any color you like just by adding a few drops of food coloring.

Preparation Time: 35 minutes
Chilling Time: 2 hours
Baking Time: 8 to 10 minutes

INGREDIENTS

1/2	CUP BUTTER *OR* MARGARINE
1/3	CUP GRANULATED SUGAR
1/4	TEASPOON BAKING POWDER
1	CUP ALL-PURPOSE FLOUR
1	OUNCE SEMISWEET CHOCOLATE, MELTED AND COOLED
1/4	TEASPOON PEPPERMINT EXTRACT
	SEVERAL DROPS FOOD COLORING (OPTIONAL)

STEPS AT A GLANCE	Page
MELTING CHOCOLATE	10
MAKING COOKIE DOUGH	8
MAKING SLICED COOKIES	68

■ In a medium mixing bowl beat the butter or margarine with an electric mixer on medium to high speed for 30 seconds. Add the sugar and baking powder; beat till combined. Beat in as much of the flour as you can with the mixer. Stir in any remaining flour with a wooden spoon. Divide dough in half.

■ Place half of the dough in a small bowl. Stir in melted chocolate, then knead dough till chocolate is evenly distributed.

■ Knead peppermint extract and, if desired, food coloring into remaining dough. Shape each half of dough into a ball. Wrap in waxed paper or plastic wrap. Chill for 2 hours, or till firm.

■ On a lightly floured surface, shape each half of dough into a log about 4 inches long. Roll and/or pat each log to a 6x3-inch rectangle. Cut each rectangle in half lengthwise, forming two 6x1½-inch rectangles. Stack all 4 rectangles on top of each other, alternating chocolate and peppermint dough. Cut the stacked layers into ¼-inch-thick slices. Place about 1 inch apart on ungreased cookie sheets.

■ Bake in a preheated 375° oven for 8 to 10 minutes, or till bottoms are a light golden brown. Remove cookies and cool on a rack.

Makes about 30 cookies

Per cookie: 54 calories, 1 g protein, 6 g carbohydrate, 3 g total fat (2 g saturated), 8 mg cholesterol, 36 mg sodium, 10 mg potassium

More cookie sleight of hand: Simply stack two contrasting doughs, then slice and bake. The layers fuse together in the oven.

Coconut-Orange Wafers

STEPS AT A GLANCE	Page
MAKING COOKIE DOUGH	8
MAKING SLICED COOKIES	68

Preparation Time: 30 minutes
Chilling Time: 2 to 3 hours
Baking Time: 7 to 9 minutes

INGREDIENTS

1/2	CUP BUTTER *OR* MARGARINE, SOFTENED
1	3-OUNCE PACKAGE CREAM CHEESE, SOFTENED
1-1/2	CUPS SIFTED POWDERED SUGAR
1/4	TEASPOON BAKING SODA
1/4	TEASPOON SALT
1	EGG
1	TABLESPOON MILK
1	TEASPOON FINELY SHREDDED ORANGE PEEL
1/4	TEASPOON COCONUT EXTRACT
2-1/2	CUPS ALL-PURPOSE FLOUR
1/2	TO 3/4 CUP TOASTED COCONUT

Two tropical flavors combine to add both taste and texture to these crisp wafers. Serve them for tea, with an iced drink, or alongside gelato or sorbet.

■ In a large mixing bowl beat the butter or margarine and cream cheese with an electric mixer on medium to high speed for 30 seconds. Add the powdered sugar, baking soda, and salt; beat till combined. Beat in the egg, milk, orange peel, and coconut extract. Beat in as much of the flour as you can with the mixer. Stir in any remaining flour with a wooden spoon. Divide dough in half. If necessary, cover and chill for 1 hour, or till dough can be shaped into rolls. Shape each half into an 8-inch roll. Roll in toasted coconut to coat all sides. Wrap each roll in waxed paper or plastic wrap. Chill for 2 hours, or till firm.

■ Cut dough into ¼-inch-thick slices. Place 2 inches apart on ungreased cookie sheets. Bake in a preheated 375° oven for 7 to 9 minutes, or till lightly browned. Remove cookies and cool on a rack.

Makes about 60 cookies

Per cookie: 50 calories, 1 g protein, 7 g carbohydrate, 2 g total fat (1 g saturated), 9 mg cholesterol, 38 mg sodium, 11 mg potassium

Get out the lounge chair, pour a tall glass of your favorite cool refresher, then set a plate of Coconut-Orange Wafers nearby.

Rocky Road Sandwich Cookies

If you love Rocky Road ice cream, wait until you try these chocolatey, marshmallowy treats. They are unusual and easy, a great combination, and the chocolate drizzle adds a whimsical final touch. For a personalized cookie, write chocolate initials on each sandwich.

■ For cookies, in a small, heavy saucepan, melt chocolate over low heat, stirring constantly. Set aside. In a large mixing bowl, beat the butter or margarine with an electric mixer on medium to high speed for 30 seconds. Add the sugar and baking powder; beat till combined. Beat in the melted chocolate, egg, and vanilla. Beat in as much of the flour as you can with the mixer. Stir in any remaining flour with a wooden spoon. Shape dough into two 7-inch rolls. Wrap in waxed paper or plastic wrap. Chill dough for 2 hours, or till firm.

■ Cut dough into slices a little less than ¼ inch thick. Place about 2 inches apart on ungreased cookie sheets. Bake in a preheated 375° oven for 8 to 10 minutes, or till edges are firm and bottoms are lightly browned. Remove cookies and cool on a rack.

■ Meanwhile, for filling, in a mixing bowl beat cream cheese and marshmallow creme with an electric mixer on medium speed till blended. Stir in walnuts, pecans, or peanuts. Spread about 2 teaspoons of the filling on bottoms of half of the cookies; top with remaining cookies.

■ If desired, for drizzle, in a small, heavy saucepan melt chocolate pieces or baking bar and shortening over low heat. Drizzle over tops of cookies. Cover and store in the refrigerator.

Makes about 32 cookies

Per cookie: 168 calories, 2 g protein, 18 g carbohydrate, 10 g total fat (7 g saturated), 28 mg cholesterol, 89 mg sodium, 46 mg potassium

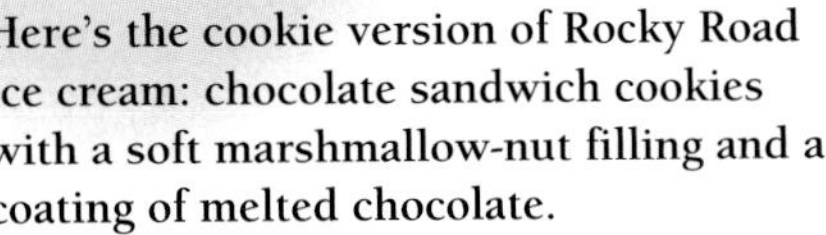

Here's the cookie version of Rocky Road ice cream: chocolate sandwich cookies with a soft marshmallow-nut filling and a coating of melted chocolate.

STEPS AT A GLANCE	Page
MELTING CHOCOLATE	10
MAKING COOKIE DOUGH	8
MAKING SLICED COOKIES	68
DRIZZLING ICING OR CHOCOLATE	11

Preparation Time: 40 minutes
Chilling Time: 2 hours
Baking Time: 8 to 10 minutes

INGREDIENTS

COOKIES

2	OUNCES SEMISWEET CHOCOLATE
1	CUP BUTTER *OR* MARGARINE, SOFTENED
3/4	CUP GRANULATED SUGAR
1	TEASPOON BAKING POWDER
1	EGG
1	TEASPOON VANILLA
2-1/2	CUPS ALL-PURPOSE FLOUR

FILLING

2	3-OUNCE PACKAGES OF CREAM CHEESE, SOFTENED
1	7-OUNCE JAR MARSHMALLOW CREME
1/2	CUP FINELY CHOPPED WALNUTS, PECANS, *OR* PEANUTS

DRIZZLE (OPTIONAL)

1/2	CUP SEMISWEET CHOCOLATE PIECES *OR* 3 OUNCES WHITE BAKING BAR, CHOPPED
1	TEASPOON SHORTENING

Shaped & Molded Cookies

Steps for Shaping and Molding Cookies

BASIC TOOLS FOR SHAPING AND MOLDING

Because your hands do much of the shaping, only these few tools are needed to prepare, mark, and bake cookie dough with simple designs.

MIXING BOWL

COOKIE SHEET AND FORK

CUTTING BOARD AND MEASURING TABLESPOON

KNIFE

COOKIE DOUGH for shaping and molding is buttery and pliable, yet tolerant of handling. It can be rolled, twisted, and formed into shapes, such as twisty pretzels or fluted cups, that are not possible to create with a cutter. This kind of dough also holds an impression. You can imprint it with simple linear patterns like the familiar crisscross used on Sesame Fork Cookies on page 94, or mold it to produce a cookie with a handsome rope edge and center medallion similar to Traditional Shortbread, page 85.

Shaped and molded cookies look best when all the cookies in a batch are similar in size and shape. Cookies will also bake more evenly if each is the same size. Take a little time to become familiar with this type of dough so you can develop just the right touch for each cookie, whether it's a delicate chocolate-dipped pirouette (see page 82) or a spicy coiled Cinnamon Snail (page 91). The steps for making balls and ropes from cookie dough as shown in this section demonstrate important basics that you will use throughout the chapter.

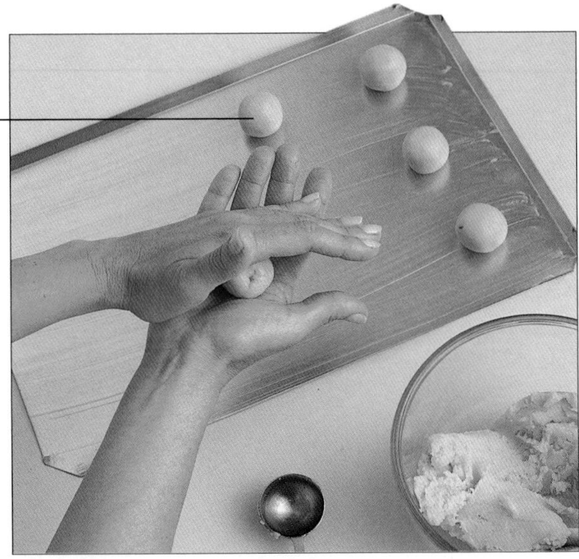

STEP 1 SHAPING BALLS

Divide the dough into equal portions of about 1 tablespoon each. Roll each portion between the palms of your hands until it is nicely rounded and smooth all over. Place the balls on lightly greased cookie sheets.

chill the dough again briefly if the fork sticks when you make the pattern

STEP 2 PRESSING WITH A FORK

Leave several inches between the dough balls. Flatten the cookies with the tines of a fork, then create crisscross lines by pressing again with the fork tines perpendicular to the first marks.

use gentle, even pressure when rolling so the rope will be uniformly thick

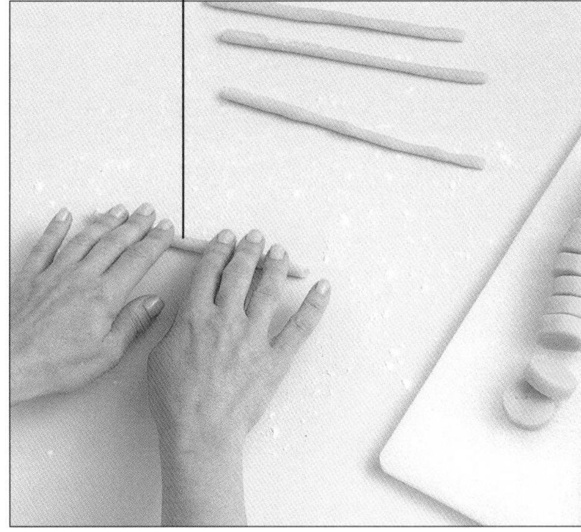

STEP 3 MAKING ROPES

Divide the dough log into ½-inch pieces. Roll each piece into a thin 8-inch rope by working it back and forth with your fingers on a lightly floured surface. As you roll the dough, work from the center out to lengthen it.

Twist lemon-scented dough into an easy pretzel shape or press into a disk and mark with a crisscrossed pattern. Lemon-Pistachio Pretzels are on page 92.

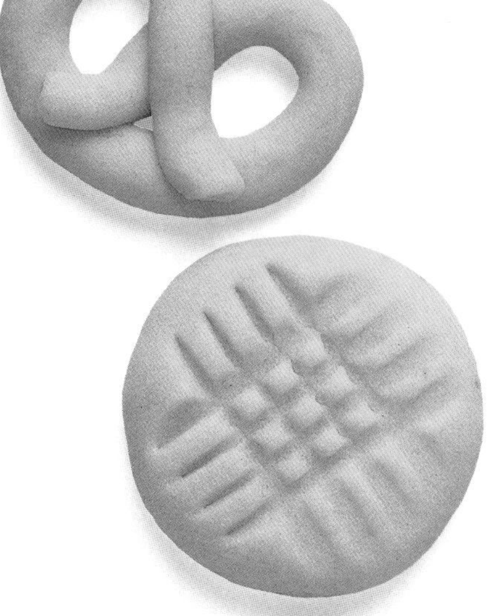

handle the rope gently to keep its rounded shape

STEP 4 SHAPING PRETZELS

Although not a true pretzel shape because it lacks the twist shown in step 5, this shape is similar and is slightly easier to accomplish. Lay one rope of dough on the baking sheet. Form a circle by crossing one end over the other, overlapping about 1 inch from the ends. Bring the ends down to the opposite edge of the circle. Press gently to seal.

twist the dough ends carefully so they don't break off

STEP 5 SHAPING TRUE PRETZELS

To make a true pretzel, form a circle with a rope of dough, crossing one end over the other about 1 inch from each end. Twist once where the rope overlaps (the dough will spiral around, and the ends of the rope will extend slightly beyond the twist).

the pressure of your hands will secure the dough ends, so it isn't necessary to seal with water in this case

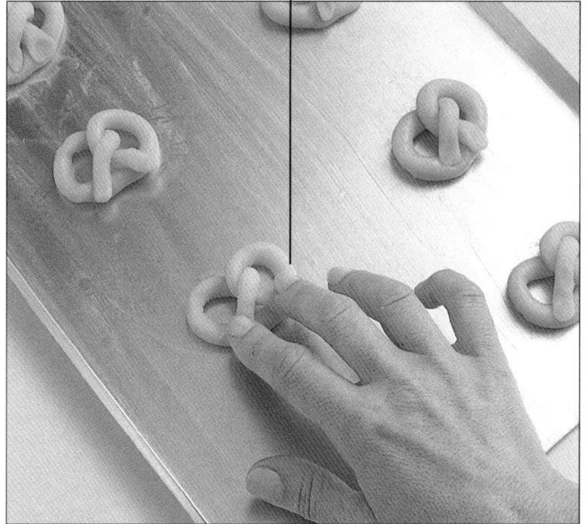

STEP 6 SECURING TWISTS

After the overlapped ends have been twisted once, lift them up from the baking sheet and set them on the opposite edge of the circle. Press down on the ends with your fingers to attach them to the dough.

Almond Crisps

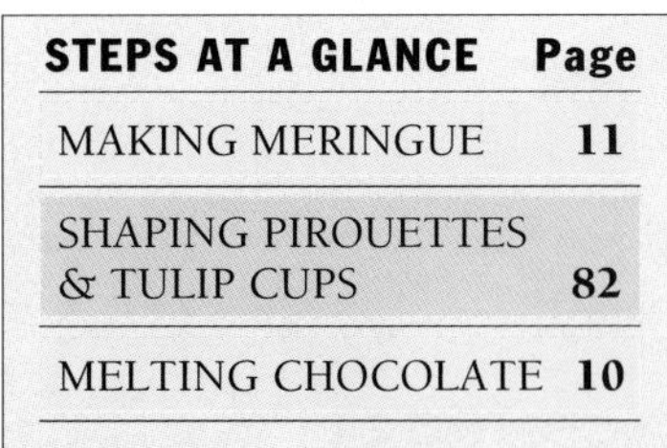

STEPS AT A GLANCE	Page
MAKING MERINGUE	11
SHAPING PIROUETTES & TULIP CUPS	82
MELTING CHOCOLATE	10

Preparation Time: 45 minutes
Baking Time: 5 to 6 minutes

INGREDIENTS

2	EGG WHITES
1/4	CUP BUTTER *OR* MARGARINE
1/2	CUP GRANULATED SUGAR
1/2	CUP ALL-PURPOSE FLOUR
1/2	TEASPOON ALMOND EXTRACT
1/2	CUP SEMISWEET CHOCOLATE PIECES (OPTIONAL)
2	TEASPOONS SHORTENING (OPTIONAL)

Roll these cookies around a spoon handle to make tubular pirouettes or place them on inverted muffin tins to create tulip cups. Dip pirouettes into melted chocolate, if desired. Fill cups with pudding, whipped cream, or ice cream, and fresh berries.

■ In a medium bowl let egg whites stand for 30 minutes at room temperature. Set aside. Generously grease a cookie sheet. (Repeat greasing cookie sheet for each batch.) Set aside. In a small saucepan heat butter or margarine over low heat just till melted. Set aside to cool.

■ Beat egg whites with an electric mixer on medium to high speed till soft peaks form (tips curl). Gradually add sugar, beating till stiff peaks form (tips stand straight). Fold in about half of the flour. Then gently stir in butter or margarine and almond extract. Fold in the remaining flour till thoroughly combined. Drop level tablespoons of batter at least 3 inches apart onto prepared cookie sheet. Spread batter into 3-inch circles. (Bake only 3 cookies at a time.) Bake in a preheated 375° oven for 5 to 6 minutes, or till cookies are golden.

■ Immediately remove a cookie from the cookie sheet. For pirouettes, place the cookie upside down on a table or countertop and quickly roll it around the greased handle of a wooden spoon or a dowel. Slide the cookie off the handle or dowel and cool on a wire rack. Or, for tulip cups, place the warm cookie on an inverted muffin tin. Working quickly, repeat with remaining warm cookies. (If cookies harden before you can shape them, reheat them in the oven for about 1 minute.)

■ To dip pirouettes, if desired, in a small, heavy saucepan heat chocolate and shortening over low heat just till melted, stirring occasionally. Remove from heat. Dip one end of each cookie into chocolate mixture. Let excess drip off. (Or, drizzle cookies with chocolate.) Transfer to a waxed paper–lined cookie sheet. Let stand till chocolate is set.

Makes about 28 cookies

Per cookie: 36 calories, 1 g protein, 5 g carbohydrate, 2 g total fat (1 g saturated), 4 mg cholesterol, 23 mg sodium, 6 mg potassium

STEPS FOR SHAPING PIROUETTES AND TULIP CUPS

STEP 1 SPREADING BATTER

For each cookie, drop 1 level tablespoon of batter onto a greased cookie sheet, then spread to a 3-inch circle with the back of a spoon.

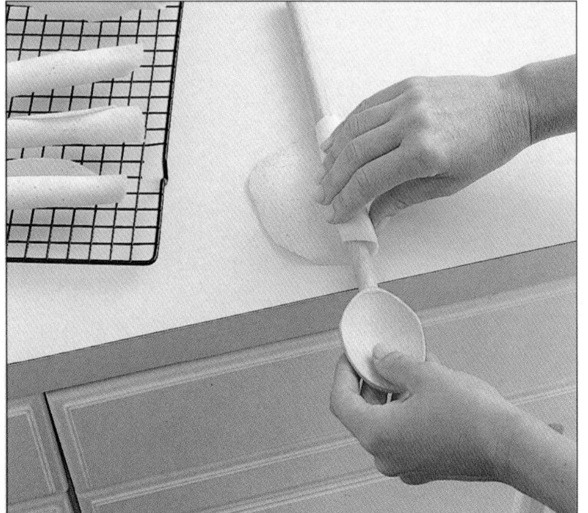

STEP 2 ROLLING PIROUETTES

Place a warm cookie upside down near the edge of a countertop or table and quickly roll it around the greased handle of a wooden spoon or a dowel. Repeat for the remaining cookies.

STEP 3 SHAPING TULIP CUPS

Invert a muffin tin and cover one cup with a warm cookie, pleating the cookie to form a cup. If the cookies harden before shaping, reheat them in the oven for about 1 minute.

Wafer-thin cookie cups and chocolate-dipped pirouettes look professionally made, but are easy to bake at home with a light, almond-flavored batter.

Made from a buttery dough, meltingly rich shortbread may be shaped by hand or in a decorative mold.

Shortbread

INGREDIENTS

1	CUP ALL-PURPOSE FLOUR
1/3	CUP GRANULATED SUGAR
1/8	TEASPOON SALT
1/2	CUP COLD BUTTER
1	TEASPOON VANILLA
	NONSTICK SPRAY COATING
	SIFTED POWDERED SUGAR (OPTIONAL)

SHORTBREAD VARIATIONS

LEMON OR ORANGE SHORTBREAD

ADD 2 TEASPOONS FINELY SHREDDED LEMON *OR* ORANGE PEEL TO THE FLOUR MIXTURE; OMIT THE VANILLA AND ADD 1/4 TEASPOON LEMON *OR* ORANGE EXTRACT

PECAN SHORTBREAD

STIR 1/4 CUP GROUND TOASTED PECANS *OR* WALNUTS IN WITH THE FLOUR MIXTURE

MOCHA SHORTBREAD

STIR 2 TABLESPOONS UNSWEETENED COCOA POWDER AND 1 TEASPOON INSTANT COFFEE CRYSTALS IN WITH THE FLOUR MIXTURE

You can hardly go anywhere in Great Britain without running into this grand staple. It is legendary in its traditional form, but we decided to come up with some variations, too, for adventuresome shortbread lovers.

■ In a medium mixing bowl stir together the flour, sugar, and salt. (For shortbread variations, adjust the flour mixture as directed.) Cut in butter till mixture resembles fine crumbs. Sprinkle with vanilla. Form the mixture into a ball and knead till smooth.

■ Spray a wooden or ceramic shortbread mold with nonstick spray coating. Firmly press the dough into the mold. Invert the mold over a lightly greased cookie sheet and tap the mold lightly to release the dough onto the cookie sheet. (If necessary, use a knife to pry the dough out of the mold.) Or, pat the dough into an 8-inch circle on a lightly greased cookie sheet. With a fork, prick dough deeply to make 8 or 16 pie-shaped wedges.

■ Bake in a preheated 325° oven for about 25 minutes, or till center of shortbread is set. While still warm, cut molded shortbread into wedges or cut hand-shaped shortbread along the perforations; remove shortbread from cookie sheet and cool completely on a rack. If desired, sprinkle wedges with powdered sugar.

Makes 8 or 16 wedges

Per wedge: 188 calories, 2 g protein, 19 g carbohydrate, 12 g total fat (7 g saturated), 31 mg cholesterol, 170 mg sodium, 21 mg potassium

Preparation Time: 15 minutes
Baking Time: 25 minutes

STEPS AT A GLANCE	Page
CUTTING IN BUTTER OR MARGARINE	34
SHAPING SHORTBREAD	85

STEPS FOR SHAPING SHORTBREAD

STEP 1 PRESSING INTO MOLD

Press the dough into a prepared mold, working from the center to the edges. Be sure the dough fills every part of the mold. Gently pry the dough out of the mold, invert onto a greased cookie sheet, and bake according to the recipe directions.

STEP 2 SHAPING BY HAND

Or, pat the dough into a circle on a greased cookie sheet. Prick the dough deeply with a fork to divide it into 8 or 16 wedges.

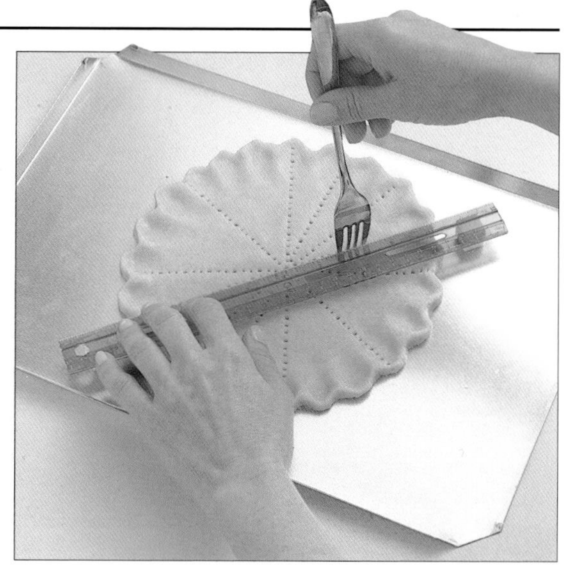

Raspberry-Orange Strips

Preparation Time: 20 minutes
Baking Time: 20 to 25 minutes

INGREDIENTS

1-1/4	CUPS ALL-PURPOSE FLOUR
3	TABLESPOONS GRANULATED SUGAR
1	TEASPOON FINELY SHREDDED ORANGE PEEL
1/2	CUP COLD BUTTER
1/4	CUP SEEDLESS RED RASPBERRY PRESERVES
1/2	CUP SLICED ALMONDS, CHOPPED PISTACHIOS, *OR* PINE NUTS

These shortbreadlike cookies are just as delicious filled with another flavor of jam or preserves. We suggest using only butter for these delectable treats. Its flavor is unmatched by any substitute.

■ In a medium mixing bowl stir together the flour, sugar, and orange peel. Cut in the butter or margarine till mixture resembles fine crumbs. Form mixture into a ball and knead till smooth. Divide dough in half.

■ Shape each portion into an 8-inch roll. Place the rolls 4 to 5 inches apart on an ungreased cookie sheet. Pat each roll into a 2-inch-wide strip. Using the back of a spoon, press a 1-inch-wide indentation lengthwise down the center of each strip. Bake in a preheated 325° oven for 20 to 25 minutes, or till edges are lightly browned. Transfer the cookie sheet to a cooling rack. Immediately spoon the preserves into the indentations. While warm, cut rectangles diagonally into 1-inch-wide pieces. Sprinkle with nuts. Cool cookies completely on cookie sheet.

Makes about 18 cookies

Per cookie: 115 calories, 2 g protein, 12 g carbohydrate, 7 g total fat (3 g saturated), 14 mg cholesterol, 53 mg sodium, 41 mg potassium

STEPS AT A GLANCE	Page
CUTTING IN BUTTER OR MARGARINE	34
MAKING STRIPS	86

STEPS FOR MAKING STRIPS

STEP 1 MAKING INDENTATIONS

Pat each roll of dough into a strip 2 inches wide. Press down the center of each strip with the back of a small spoon to create a 1-inch-wide indentation.

STEP 2 CUTTING STRIPS

Bake the strips, transfer to a wire rack, then immediately fill the indentations with preserves. While the strips are still warm, cut them diagonally with a sharp knife into 1-inch-wide pieces. Sprinkle with nuts and cool completely.

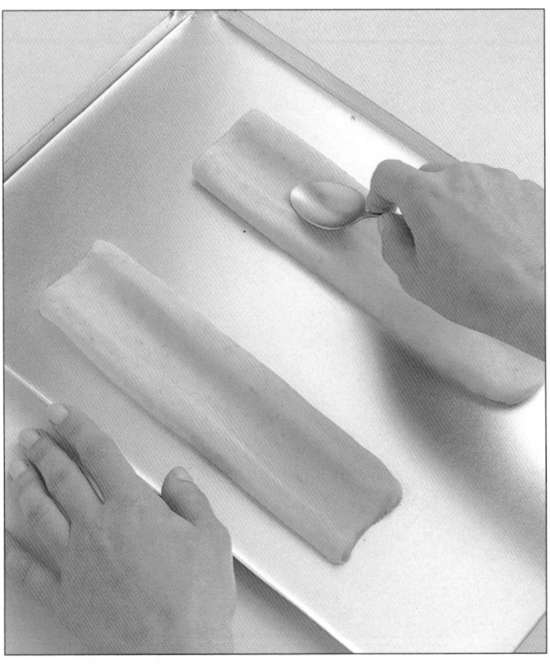

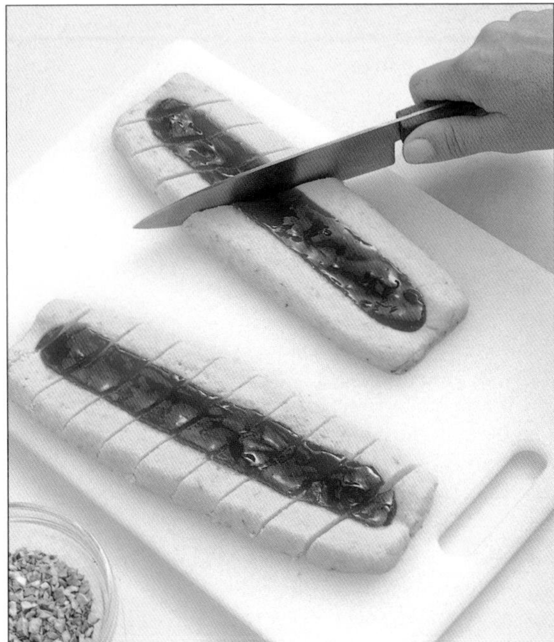

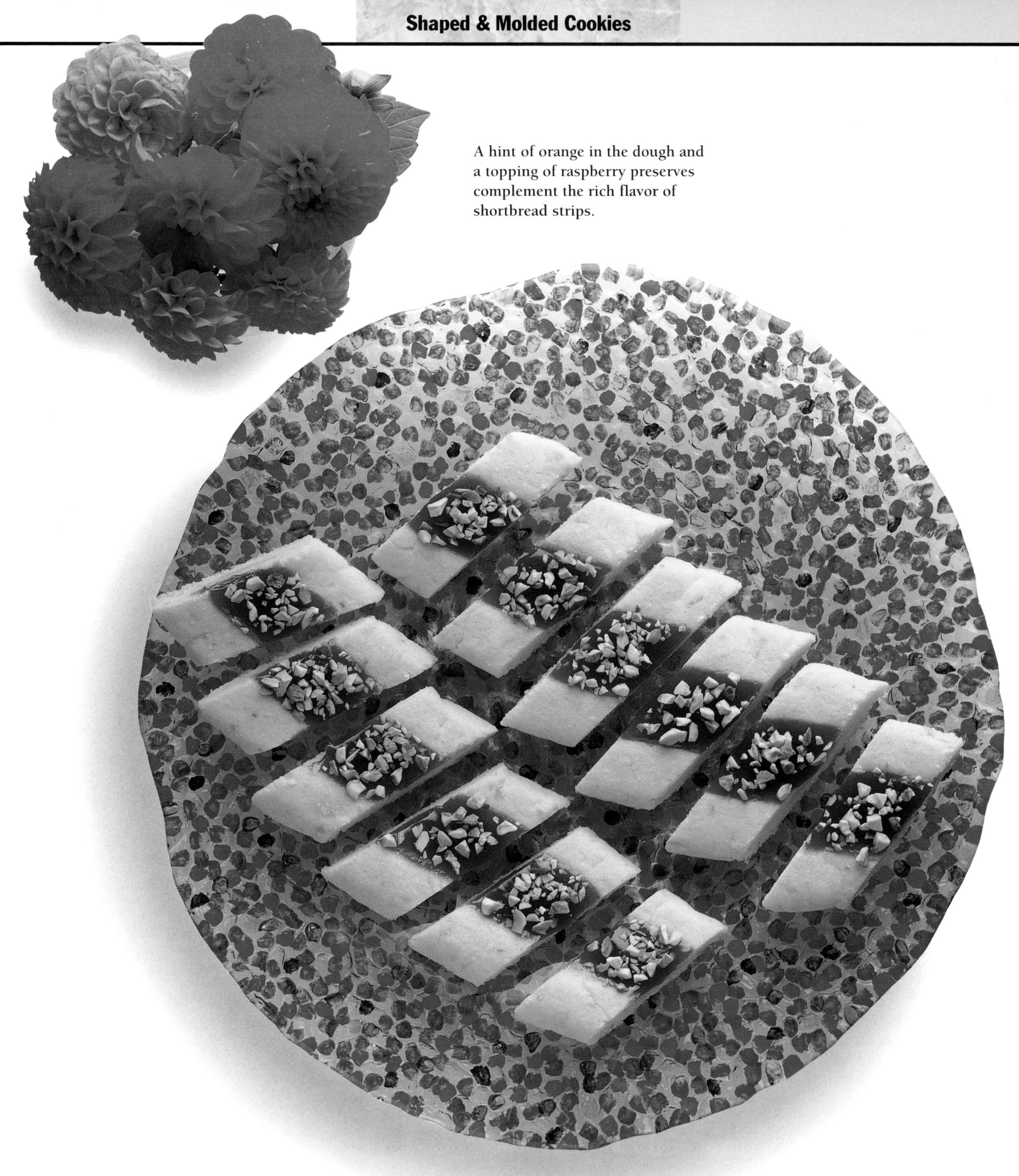

A hint of orange in the dough and a topping of raspberry preserves complement the rich flavor of shortbread strips.

Chocolate-Kahlúa Truffle Cookies

Thin drizzles of white and semisweet chocolate are easily applied to these coated cookies by letting the melted topping fall from the tip of a spoon in a zigzag pattern.

Preparation Time: 1 hour
Chilling Time: 30 minutes

INGREDIENTS

2-1/2	CUPS FINELY CRUSHED CHOCOLATE WAFERS (ABOUT 45 WAFERS)
1	CUP FINELY CHOPPED WALNUTS, PECANS, PINE NUTS, ALMONDS, *OR* HAZELNUTS
1	CUP SIFTED POWDERED SUGAR
1/3	CUP KAHLÚA *OR* OTHER COFFEE LIQUEUR
1	TO 2 TABLESPOONS WATER
5	OUNCES SEMISWEET CHOCOLATE, CHOPPED
1	TABLESPOON SHORTENING
6	OUNCES WHITE BAKING BAR, CHOPPED

These candylike no-bake cookies are quick, easy, and impressive, and almost any of your favorite liqueurs may be used to make them. Try hazelnut, orange, Irish cream, or chocolate flavors.

■ In a large mixing bowl stir together the chocolate wafer crumbs, chopped nuts, powdered sugar, and Kahlúa or other liqueur. Add enough of the water so crumbs hold together. Shape mixture into 1-inch balls. Place on a waxed paper–lined cookie sheet.

■ In a small, heavy saucepan heat semisweet chocolate and shortening over low heat till melted. In another small, heavy saucepan heat white baking bar till melted. With a fork, dip half of the cookies into the semisweet chocolate mixture to coat; place on cookie sheet. Dip remaining cookies in melted white baking bar to coat; place on cookie sheet.

■ With the tip of a spoon, thinly drizzle white baking bar mixture in a zigzag pattern over cookies coated with semisweet chocolate. Repeat with semisweet chocolate, drizzling over cookies coated with white baking bar mixture. Refrigerate for about 30 minutes, or till chocolate is firm. Store in refrigerator.

Makes about 30 cookies

Per cookie: 147 calories, 2 g protein, 18 g carbohydrate, 7 g total fat (2 g saturated), 1 mg cholesterol, 72 mg sodium, 58 mg potassium

STEPS AT A GLANCE	Page
SHAPING BALLS	80
MELTING CHOCOLATE	10
DRIZZLING ICING OR CHOCOLATE	11

Pecan Florentines

These lacy cookies are buttery and crisp. Don't bake more than 5 cookies on the cookie sheet at one time because even a tiny amount of cookie batter will spread a lot.

■ Line cookie sheets with foil. Grease the foil. Set cookie sheets aside.

■ In a medium mixing bowl stir together the sugar, melted butter or margarine, molasses, and milk. Stir in the ground pecans or walnuts and flour.

■ Drop level teaspoons of batter 5 inches apart onto a prepared cookie sheet. (Bake only 3 to 5 cookies at a time.) Bake in a preheated 350° oven for 5 to 6 minutes, or till bubbly and deep golden brown. Cool cookies on cookie sheet for 1 to 2 minutes, or till set. Quickly remove cookies from pan and cool on a rack. Repeat to bake remaining cookies.

■ In a small, heavy saucepan melt chocolate or white baking bar over low heat. Drizzle over cookies.

Makes about 36 cookies

Per cookie: 90 calories, 1 g protein, 10 g carbohydrate, 5 g total fat (1 g saturated), 3 mg cholesterol, 68 mg sodium, 22 mg potassium

INGREDIENTS

1/4	CUP GRANULATED SUGAR
1/4	CUP BUTTER *OR* MARGARINE, MELTED
1	TABLESPOON MOLASSES
1	TABLESPOON MILK
1/4	CUP GROUND PECANS *OR* WALNUTS
1/4	CUP ALL-PURPOSE FLOUR
1/2	OF A 4-OUNCE PACKAGE SWEET BAKING CHOCOLATE *OR* 2 OUNCES WHITE BAKING BAR

Preparation Time: 20 minutes
Baking Time: 5 to 6 minutes

STEPS AT A GLANCE	Page
GRINDING NUTS	18
DRIZZLING ICING OR CHOCLATE	11

As they bake, teaspoonfuls of nutty, caramel-colored batter spread into large, lacy cookies that become crisp and shiny when cool.

Peanut Butter Bonbons

INGREDIENTS

1/2	CUP BUTTER *OR* MARGARINE, SOFTENED
1/2	CUP CHUNKY PEANUT BUTTER
3/4	CUP PACKED BROWN SUGAR
1/4	TEASPOON BAKING SODA
1	EGG
1-1/2	TEASPOONS VANILLA
2-1/2	CUPS ALL-PURPOSE FLOUR
1	12-OUNCE PACKAGE SEMISWEET CHOCOLATE PIECES
2	TEASPOONS SHORTENING

Preparation Time: 30 minutes
Baking Time: 8 to 10 minutes

STEPS AT A GLANCE	Page
MAKING COOKIE DOUGH	8
SHAPING BALLS	80
MELTING CHOCOLATE	10

We call these bonbons because they have the look and richness of melt-in-your-mouth candy, but they are a snap to make.

■ In a large mixing bowl beat the butter or margarine and peanut butter with an electric mixer on medium to high speed for 30 seconds. Add the brown sugar and baking soda; beat till combined. Beat in the egg and vanilla. Beat in as much of the flour as you can with the mixer. Stir in any remaining flour with a wooden spoon.

■ Shape dough into 1-inch balls. Place balls 1½ inches apart on ungreased cookie sheets.

■ Bake in a preheated 350° oven for 8 to 10 minutes, or till cookies are set and lightly browned on the bottom. Remove cookies from pan and cool on a rack.

■ In a medium, heavy saucepan heat chocolate and shortening over low heat till melted. Cool slightly. Using a fork, dip peanut butter balls, one at a time, into chocolate mixture to coat. Transfer to waxed paper–lined cookie sheets. Chill till firm. Store in a cool place.

Makes about 52 bonbons

Per bonbon: 96 calories, 2 g protein, 12 g carbohydrate, 5 g total fat (1 g saturated), 9 mg cholesterol, 41 mg sodium, 58 mg potassium

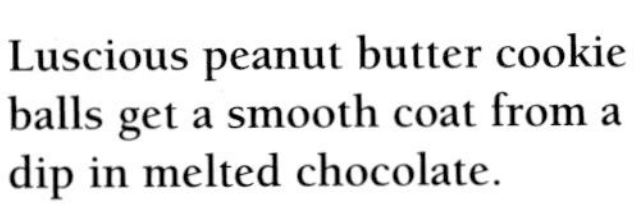

Luscious peanut butter cookie balls get a smooth coat from a dip in melted chocolate.

Cinnamon Snails

Preparation Time: 20 minutes
Baking Time: 8 minutes

INGREDIENTS

3/4	CUP BUTTER *OR* MARGARINE, SOFTENED
3/4	CUP PACKED BROWN SUGAR
1	TEASPOON GROUND CINNAMON
1/4	TEASPOON BAKING POWDER
1	EGG
1	TEASPOON VANILLA
2	CUPS ALL-PURPOSE FLOUR
1	TABLESPOON GRANULATED SUGAR
1/2	TEASPOON GROUND CINNAMON
1	SLIGHTLY BEATEN EGG WHITE
96	MINIATURE SEMISWEET CHOCOLATE PIECES (OPTIONAL)

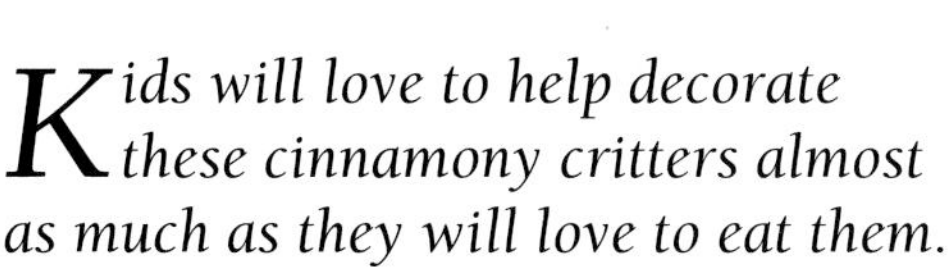

Kids will love to help decorate these cinnamony critters almost as much as they will love to eat them.

■ In a mixing bowl beat the butter or margarine with an electric mixer on medium to high speed for 30 seconds. Add the brown sugar, 1 teaspoon cinnamon, and baking powder; beat till combined. Beat in the egg and vanilla. Beat in as much of the flour as you can with the mixer. Stir in any remaining flour with a wooden spoon. Divide dough in half.

■ In a small mixing bowl stir together the granulated sugar and ½ teaspoon cinnamon. Set aside.

■ On a lightly floured surface, shape each half of the dough into a 12-inch log. Cut each log into twenty-four ½-inch pieces. Roll each piece into a 6-inch rope. Coil each rope into a snail shape; using one end to make a small coil for the eye, and coiling the other end in the opposite direction to make the body. Place the cookies 2 inches apart on lightly greased cookie sheets. Brush each cookie with egg white. Sprinkle with sugar-cinnamon mixture. If desired, insert 2 chocolate pieces in the small coiled end for the eyes.

■ Bake in a preheated 375° oven for 8 minutes, or till edges of the cookies are firm and the bottoms are lightly browned. Remove cookies from pan and cool on a rack.

Makes about 48 cookies

Per cookie: 59 calories, 1 g protein, 7 g carbohydrate, 3 g total fat (2 g saturated), 12 mg cholesterol, 36 mg sodium, 20 mg potassium

Brown-sugar cookie "snails," shaped by hand and decorated with chocolate-chip "eyes," make delightful treats for children.

STEPS AT A GLANCE	Page
MAKING COOKIE DOUGH	8
MAKING ROPES	81

Lemon-Pistachio Pretzels

Preparation Time: 25 minutes
Chilling Time: 30 to 60 minutes
Baking Time: 8 to 10 minutes

INGREDIENTS

3/4	CUP BUTTER *OR* MARGARINE, SOFTENED
1	CUP SIFTED POWDERED SUGAR
2	TEASPOONS FINELY SHREDDED LEMON PEEL
1	EGG
1/2	TEASPOON LEMON EXTRACT
2	CUPS ALL-PURPOSE FLOUR
1-1/2	CUPS SIFTED POWDERED SUGAR
1	TABLESPOON LEMON JUICE
1	TO 2 TABLESPOONS WATER
1/3	CUP FINELY CHOPPED PISTACHIOS, WALNUTS, *OR* ALMONDS

Sweet, buttery cookie pretzels are smoothly glazed with a lemon icing, then sprinkled with chopped pistachios for textural contrast.

If you want to make these sweet pretzels even more delicate, grind the nuts in a blender or food processor instead of just chopping them.

■ In a mixing bowl beat the butter or margarine with an electric mixer on medium to high speed for 30 seconds. Add 1 cup powdered sugar and lemon peel; beat till combined. Beat in the egg and lemon extract. Beat in as much of the flour as you can with the mixer. Stir in any remaining flour with a wooden spoon. Divide dough in half. If necessary, cover and chill for 30 to 60 minutes, or till dough is easy to handle.

■ On a lightly floured surface, shape each half of the dough into a 12-inch log. Cut each log into twenty-four ½-inch pieces. Roll each piece into an 8-inch rope. Form each rope into a pretzel shape by crossing one end over the other to form a circle, overlapping them about 1 inch from each end. Twist once at the point where dough overlaps. Lift ends across to the edge of the circle opposite them and press lightly to seal. Place about 2 inches apart on lightly greased cookie sheets.

■ Bake in a preheated 375° oven for 8 to 10 minutes, or till light golden brown.

■ In a small bowl stir together 1½ cups powdered sugar, lemon juice, and enough water to make a mixture of glazing consistency. Brush cookies with glaze; sprinkle with pistachios or other nuts. Let stand till set.

Makes about 48 cookies

Per cookie: 78 calories, 1 g protein, 11 g carbohydrate, 3 g total fat (2 g saturated), 12 mg cholesterol, 35 mg sodium, 17 mg potassium

STEPS AT A GLANCE	Page
MAKING COOKIE DOUGH	8
SHAPING PRETZELS	81

Koulourakia

When visiting a Greek home, you might be welcomed with this licorice-flavored cookie along with a small cup of strong coffee and a glass of cold water.

■ In a large mixing bowl beat the butter or margarine with an electric mixer on medium to high speed for 30 seconds. Add the sugar, baking powder, aniseed, and lemon peel; beat till combined. Beat in the eggs and 2 tablespoons milk. Beat in as much of the flour as you can with the mixer. Stir in any remaining flour with a wooden spoon. Divide dough in half. If necessary, chill dough for 30 to 60 minutes, or till easy to handle.

■ On a lightly floured surface, shape each half of dough into a 12-inch log. Cut each log into twenty-four ½-inch pieces. Roll each piece into a 6-inch rope. Curl each end of the rope to form an S shape. Place the cookies 1 inch apart on greased cookie sheets.

■ In a small mixing bowl stir together egg white and 1 tablespoon milk; brush mixture over cookies. If desired, sprinkle with sesame seed.

■ Bake in a preheated 375° oven for 7 to 9 minutes, or till bottoms are lightly browned. Remove cookies from pans and cool on a rack.

Makes about 48 cookies

Per cookie: 67 calories, 1 g protein, 9 g carbohydrate, 3 g total fat (1 g saturated), 19 mg cholesterol, 39 mg sodium, 15 mg potassium

INGREDIENTS

- 3/4 CUP BUTTER *OR* MARGARINE, SOFTENED
- 3/4 CUP GRANULATED SUGAR
- 2 TEASPOONS BAKING POWDER
- 1 TEASPOON ANISEED
- 1 TEASPOON FINELY SHREDDED LEMON PEEL
- 2 EGGS
- 2 TABLESPOONS MILK
- 3 CUPS ALL-PURPOSE FLOUR
- 1 SLIGHTLY BEATEN EGG WHITE
- 1 TABLESPOON MILK
- 3 TABLESPOONS SESAME SEED (OPTIONAL)

Preparation Time: 30 minutes
Chilling Time: 30 to 60 minutes
Baking Time: 7 to 9 minutes

STEPS AT A GLANCE	Page
MAKING COOKIE DOUGH	8
MAKING ROPES	81

Letter-shaped cookies like these anise-flavored ones from Greece are also traditional in Scandinavia.

Sesame Fork Cookies

Preparation Time: 35 minutes
Baking Time: 7 to 9 minutes

INGREDIENTS

3/4	CUP BUTTER *OR* MARGARINE, SOFTENED
1	CUP PACKED BROWN SUGAR
1-1/2	TEASPOONS BAKING POWDER
1/4	TEASPOON GROUND NUTMEG
1	EGG
3	TABLESPOONS TAHINI (SESAME PASTE) *OR* PEANUT BUTTER
1	TEASPOON VANILLA
1	CUP WHOLE WHEAT FLOUR
1-2/3	CUPS ALL-PURPOSE FLOUR
1/3	CUP SESAME SEED

STEPS AT A GLANCE	Page
MAKING COOKIE DOUGH	8
SHAPING BALLS	80
PRESSING WITH A FORK	81

These may look like old-fashioned peanut butter cookies, but their texture and flavor is deliciously updated with tahini (sesame paste).

■ In a large mixing bowl beat the butter or margarine with an electric mixer on medium to high speed for 30 seconds. Add the brown sugar, baking powder, and nutmeg; beat till combined. Beat in the egg, tahini or peanut butter, and vanilla. Beat in the whole-wheat flour and as much of the all-purpose flour as you can with the mixer. Stir in any remaining all-purpose flour and the sesame seed with a wooden spoon. Shape dough into 1-inch balls. Place 2 inches apart on ungreased cookie sheets. Flatten each ball by pressing with the tines of a fork in a crisscross pattern.

■ Bake in a preheated 375° oven for 7 to 9 minutes, or till lightly browned. Remove cookies from the pans and cool on a rack.

Makes about 70 cookies

Per cookie: 52 calories, 1 g protein, 7 g carbohydrate, 3 g total fat (1 g saturated), 8 mg cholesterol, 26 mg sodium, 27 mg potassium

Tahini instead of the usual peanut butter adds an exotic, unexpected flavor to these easily prepared tea cookies.

Pressed Cookies

Steps for Making Pressed Cookies

Basic Tools for Making Pressed Cookies

For pressed cookies, you need the standard equipment for making and baking dough, plus an easy-to-operate press that comes with an assortment of removable design plates.

MIXING BOWL

COOKIE SHEET AND SMALL, SHARP KNIFE

RUBBER SPATULA

COOKIE PRESS AND PLATES

Pressed, or "spritz," cookies are an old Scandinavian specialty, but they have become a favorite in many other countries, too. Most cookie presses are simple devices that operate with either a lever-and-ratchet system or with a rotating screw top (an electric press is also available, but is a little more difficult to find). A removable coupler at the bottom of the container holds your choice of interchangeable design plates and, in some cases, plain or star-shaped tips. To use, secure the plate or tip, pack the dough into the container, and force it through the press onto an ungreased cookie sheet. Out come little wreaths, miniature trees, dainty butterflies, delicate flowers, ridged ribbons, or any one of the dozens of patterns created by the manufacturer. The press does all the work and does it perfectly. All you do is make the dough, choose the design, and bake the result. As the shapes themselves are so decorative, the only finishing touch might be a sprinkling of glittering sugar crystals, a scattering of finely chopped nuts, or a chocolate tint in the dough. Always use room-temperature dough, as chilled dough is too stiff to push through the press easily.

drop the plate in so that it rests flat in the holder

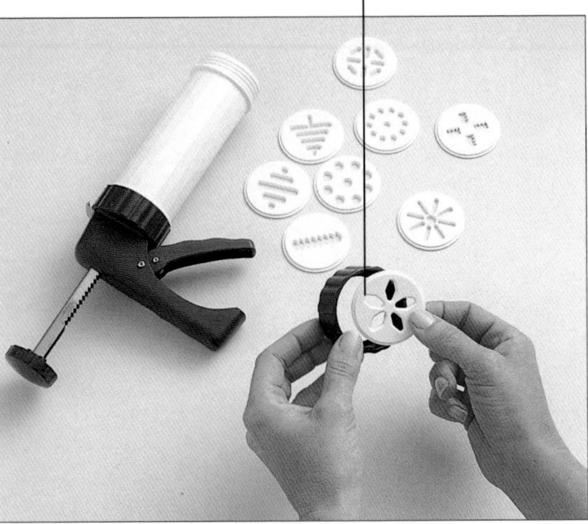

some recipes call for using a plain or star-shaped tip, which is also dropped into the holder

STEP 1 Putting Plate in Holder

Unscrew the holder from the bottom of the cookie press. Place a plate in the holder with the correct side facing up (as specified by the manufacturer's directions).

for a narrow press, use a narrow spatula to transfer the dough

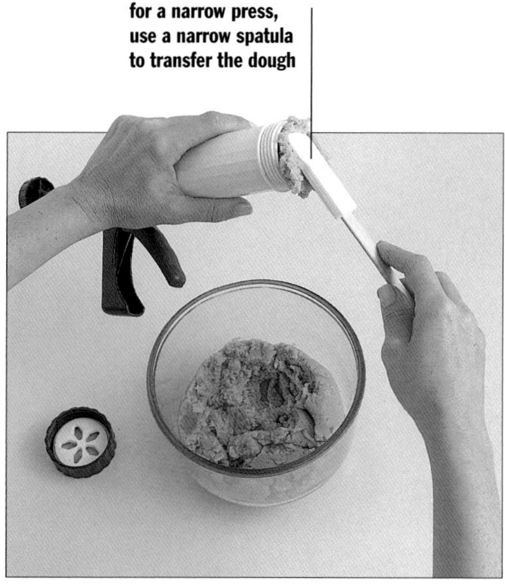

don't let the dough squeeze out under the press

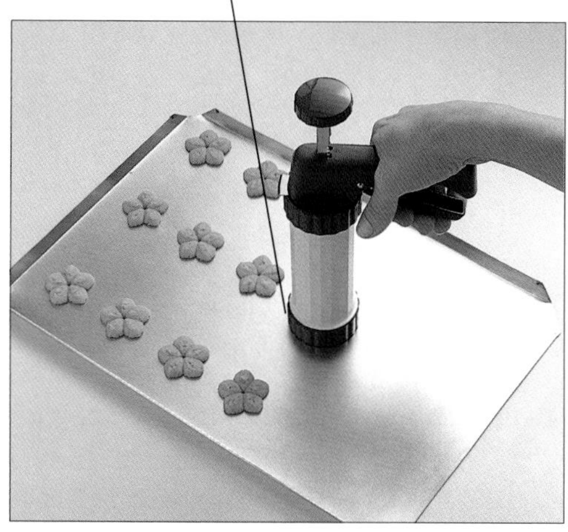

lift up the press when the cookie is the desired length

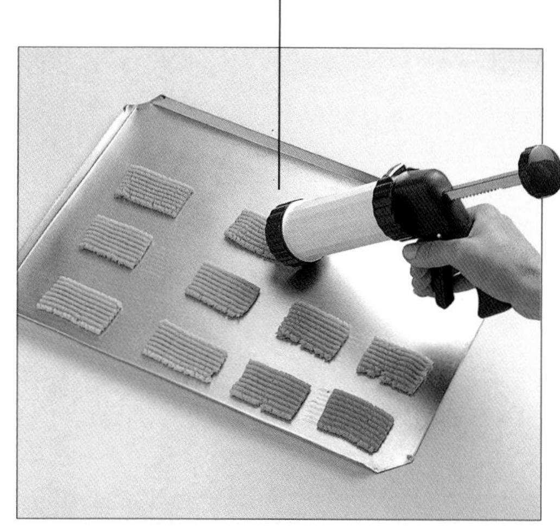

STEP 2 PACKING PRESS WITH DOUGH

Scoop up cookie dough with a rubber spatula and pack it into the container of the press. Don't leave any large air holes in the dough or the shapes will distort when pressed out. Screw on the holder and plate or tip.

STEP 3 FORCING DOUGH THROUGH PRESS

For all shapes except ribbons (see step 4), hold the press straight down on an ungreased cookie sheet. Force the dough through (it will stick to the cookie sheet) and release the pressure just before you lift the press off the cookie.

STEP 4 MAKING RIBBONS

Hold the press at an angle. Draw the press along the ungreased cookie sheet in a straight line as you force out the dough.

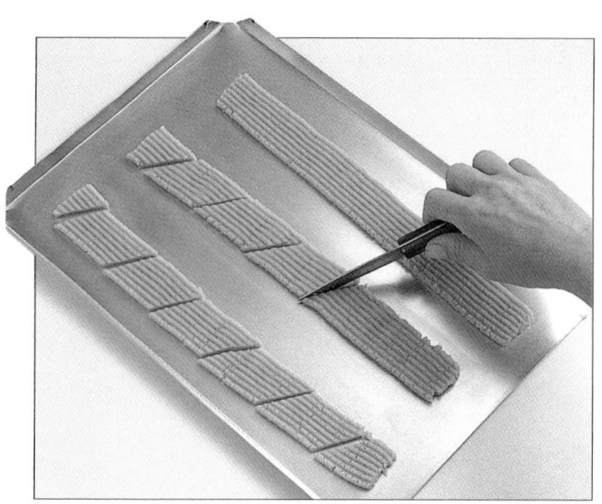

you can also cut strips with a rolling pastry wheel for straight or fluted edges

STEP 5 MAKING DIAGONAL RIBBONS

Press out long strips of dough onto the cookie sheet. Use a sharp knife to cut the strips at an angle, being careful not to cut too deeply so you will not mark the cookie sheet.

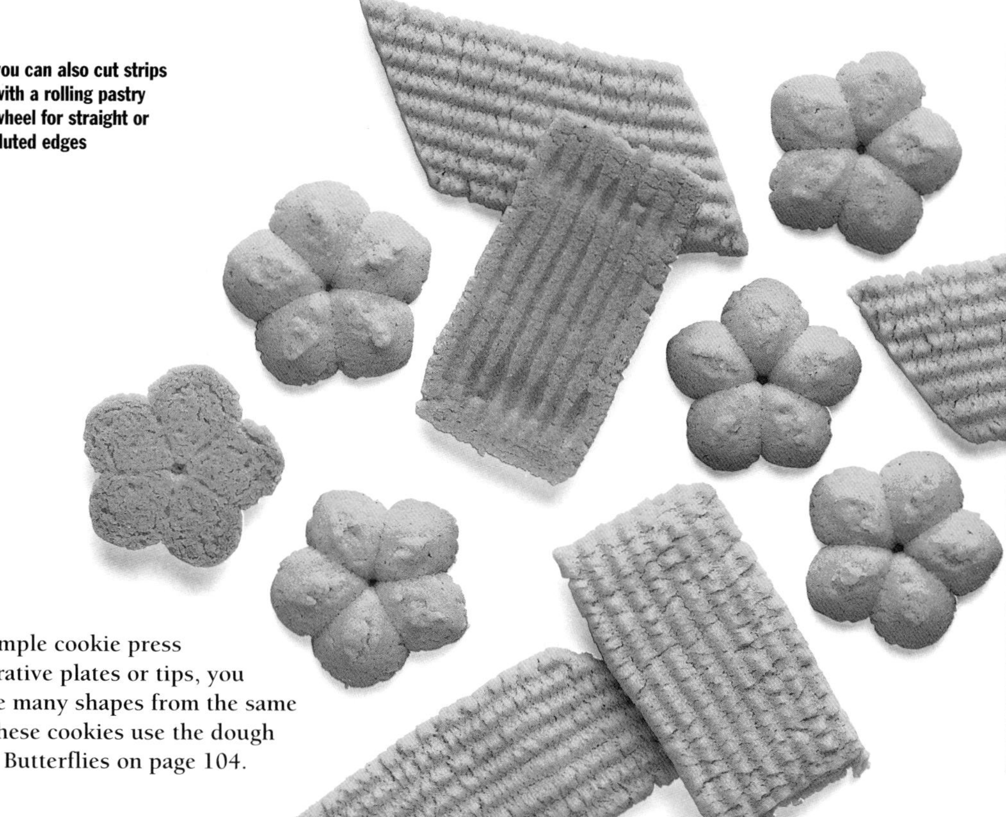

With a simple cookie press and decorative plates or tips, you can create many shapes from the same dough. These cookies use the dough for Anise Butterflies on page 104.

Almond Half-Moons

STEPS AT A GLANCE	Page
MAKING COOKIE DOUGH	8
MAKING PRESSED COOKIES	96
SHAPING HALF-MOONS	98

Preparation Time: 30 minutes
Baking Time: 6 to 8 minutes

INGREDIENTS

1	CUP BUTTER *OR* MARGARINE, SOFTENED
1/2	CUP GRANULATED SUGAR
1	EGG
1/4	TEASPOON ALMOND EXTRACT
2-1/4	CUPS ALL-PURPOSE FLOUR
3/4	CUP GROUND ALMONDS, HAZELNUTS, *OR* PECANS
	SIFTED POWDERED SUGAR

These crisp little cookies, reminiscent of Chinese almond cookies, will taste great in any shape your cookie press makes, but be sure to choose a tip with at least a ½-inch opening — the ground nuts might get caught in a smaller opening.

■ In a large mixing bowl beat the butter or margarine with an electric mixer on medium to high speed for 30 seconds. Add the sugar; beat till combined. Beat in the egg and almond extract. Beat in as much of the flour as you can with the mixer. Stir in any remaining flour and the ground nuts with a wooden spoon. Do not chill dough.

■ Pack dough into a cookie press fitted with a ½-inch-wide round or star tip. Force dough through the cookie press 1 inch apart onto ungreased cookie sheets forming crescent shapes.

■ Bake in a preheated 375° oven for 6 to 8 minutes, or till edges are firm and bottoms are lightly browned. Remove cookies from pans and cool on a rack. Sprinkle cookies with powdered sugar.

Makes about 70 cookies

Per cookie: 52 calories, 1 g protein, 5 g carbohydrate, 3 g total fat (2 g saturated), 10 mg cholesterol, 32 mg sodium, 16 mg potassium

STEPS FOR SHAPING HALF-MOONS

STEP 1 BENDING DOUGH

Press out 3 long strips of dough on an ungreased cookie sheet through a ½-inch tip. Cut each strip into 2½-inch lengths. To make a half-moon, press a finger in the middle of one length of dough while pushing the ends in the other direction.

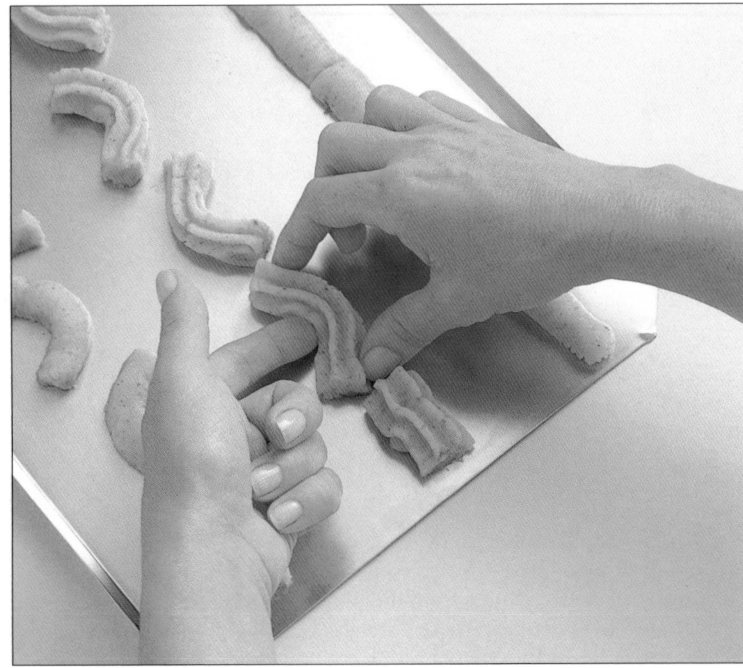

The ridged half-moons were shaped with a cookie press fitted with a star tip, while the smooth ones were made with a plain tip.

The bumpy cracks and crevices of festive spritz cookies trap chunks of nuts and bits of decorative chocolate sprinkles.

Chocolate Butter Spritz

If you're in a hurry, you can also make these as drop cookies simply by dropping rounded teaspoonfuls of the dough onto the cookie sheets.

■ In a large mixing bowl beat the butter or margarine with an electric mixer on medium to high speed for 30 seconds. Add the powdered sugar, brown sugar, and cocoa powder; beat till combined. Beat in the egg yolk, crème de cacao or milk, and vanilla. Beat in as much of the flour as you can with the mixer. Stir in any remaining flour with a wooden spoon. Do not chill dough.

■ Pack the dough into a cookie press fitted with desired plate. Force dough through press 1 inch apart onto ungreased cookie sheets. If desired, sprinkle with chocolate sprinkles or chopped nuts.

■ Bake in a preheated 375° oven for 8 to 10 minutes, or till edges of cookies are firm but not brown. Remove cookies from pans and cool on a rack.

Makes about 60 cookies

Per cookie: 58 calories, 1 g protein, 7 g carbohydrate, 3 g total fat (2 g saturated), 9 mg cholesterol, 37 mg sodium, 13 mg potassium

STEPS AT A GLANCE	**Page**
MAKING COOKIE DOUGH	**8**
MAKING PRESSED COOKIES	**96**
DECORATING SPRITZ COOKIES	**101**

Preparation Time: 25 minutes
Baking Time: 8 to 10 minutes

INGREDIENTS

1	CUP BUTTER *OR* MARGARINE, SOFTENED
1/2	CUP SIFTED POWDERED SUGAR
1/2	CUP PACKED BROWN SUGAR
1/4	CUP UNSWEETENED COCOA POWDER
1	EGG YOLK
2	TABLESPOONS CRÈME DE CACAO *OR* MILK
1	TEASPOON VANILLA
2-1/3	CUPS ALL-PURPOSE FLOUR
	CHOCOLATE SPRINKLES *OR* FINELY CHOPPED NUTS (OPTIONAL)

STEPS FOR DECORATING SPRITZ COOKIES

STEP 1 SPRINKLING

Prepare the chocolate dough and pack it into a cookie press. Press out cookies onto ungreased cookie sheets using one or more decorative plates. Sprinkle the unbaked cookies with chocolate sprinkles or finely chopped nuts. As the cookies bake, the toppings will stick to them.

Glazed Almond Strips

INGREDIENTS

3/4	CUP BUTTER *OR* MARGARINE, SOFTENED
1/2	CUP PACKED BROWN SUGAR
2	TEASPOONS MILK
	FEW DROPS ALMOND EXTRACT
1-3/4	CUPS ALL-PURPOSE FLOUR
1	SLIGHTLY BEATEN EGG WHITE
1/2	CUP SLICED ALMONDS *OR* PINE NUTS
1	TEASPOON GRANULATED SUGAR

As an alternative to making several 2½-inch strips with the cookie press, you can make one long strip and then cut it into the correct lengths with a knife.

■ In a mixing bowl beat the butter or margarine with an electric mixer on medium to high speed for 30 seconds. Add the brown sugar, milk, and almond extract; beat till combined. Mix in as much of the flour as you can with the mixer. Stir in any remaining flour with a wooden spoon. Do not chill dough.

■ Pack the dough into a cookie press fitted with a ribbon plate. Force dough through cookie press onto ungreased cookie sheets, making 2½-inch ribbons about 1 inch apart. Using a pastry brush, brush each cookie with egg white, then sprinkle with almonds or pine nuts and granulated sugar.

■ Bake in a preheated 375° oven for 7 to 8 minutes, or till edges are firm but not brown. Let cool 1 minute on cookie sheets. Remove cookies from pans and cool on a rack.

Makes about 54 cookies

Per cookie: 50 calories, 1 g protein, 5 g carbohydrate, 3 g total fat (2 g saturated), 7 mg cholesterol, 32 mg sodium, 21 mg potassium

Preparation Time: 30 minutes
Baking Time: 7 to 8 minutes

STEPS AT A GLANCE	Page
MAKING COOKIE DOUGH	8
MAKING PRESSED COOKIES	96
MAKING ALMOND STRIPS	102

STEPS FOR MAKING ALMOND STRIPS

STEP 1 BRUSHING GLAZE
Slightly beat the egg white and brush it on each cookie with a pastry brush, making sure that it fills the ridges. The glaze will give the cookies a subtle sheen and will serve as "glue" for the nut topping.

STEP 2 ADDING ALMONDS
After the cookies have been brushed with egg white, arrange almonds decoratively on each. If desired, the design can differ from cookie to cookie. Sprinkle with sugar, and bake.

These old-fashioned "washboard" cookies were easily formed with a cookie press fitted with a ribbon plate, then decorated with glistening sugar crystals and almonds.

Anise Butterflies

STEPS AT A GLANCE	Page
MAKING COOKIE DOUGH	8
MAKING PRESSED COOKIES	96

Preparation Time: 15 minutes
Baking Time: 8 to 10 minutes

INGREDIENTS

3/4	CUP BUTTER *OR* MARGARINE, SOFTENED
1/2	CUP PACKED BROWN SUGAR
1/2	TEASPOON BAKING POWDER
1/4	TEASPOON GROUND CINNAMON
1/8	TEASPOON GROUND GINGER
1	EGG YOLK
1	TEASPOON ANISE EXTRACT
1-3/4	CUPS ALL-PURPOSE FLOUR

Butterflies and other fanciful designs are easy to make with a cookie press.

Making spritz cookies will go more smoothly if you pack the dough firmly into the cookie press. This eliminates any air pockets that could leave holes in the shapes.

■ In a large mixing bowl beat the butter or margarine with an electric mixer on medium to high speed for 30 seconds. Add the brown sugar, baking powder, cinnamon, and ginger; beat till combined. Beat in the egg yolk and anise extract. Beat in as much of the flour as you can with the mixer. Stir in any remaining flour with a wooden spoon. Do not chill dough.

■ Pack the dough into a cookie press fitted with a butterfly plate. Force dough through press 1 inch apart onto ungreased cookie sheets.

■ Bake in a preheated 375° oven for 8 to 10 minutes, or till edges of cookies are firm but not brown. Remove cookies from pans and cool on a rack.

Makes about 60 cookies

Per cookie: 41 calories, 0 g protein, 4 g carbohydrate, 2 g total fat (1 g saturated), 10 mg cholesterol, 28 mg sodium, 12 mg potassium

Lemon-Ginger Tea Cookies

STEPS AT A GLANCE	Page
MAKING COOKIE DOUGH	8
MAKING PRESSED COOKIES	96

Don't use cookie-press plates with very small openings for this recipe; the lemon peel and ginger slivers may clog up the openings.

■ In a mixing bowl beat the butter or margarine with an electric mixer on medium to high speed for 30 seconds. Add the sugar, lemon peel, ginger, and cloves; beat till combined. Beat in the egg and lemon juice till combined. Beat in as much of the flour as you can with the mixer. Stir in any remaining flour with a wooden spoon. Do not chill dough.

■ Pack dough into a cookie press fitted with the desired plate. Force dough 1 inch apart onto ungreased cookie sheets. If desired, decorate cookies with slivered crystallized ginger and/or candied lemon peel.

■ Bake in a preheated 375° oven for 8 to 10 minutes, or till edges are set and beginning to brown. Remove cookies from pans and cool on a rack.

Makes about 100 cookies

Per cookie: 47 calories, 1 g protein, 5 g carbohydrate, 3 g total fat (2 g saturated), 9 mg cholesterol, 33 mg sodium, 7 mg potassium

Preparation Time: 20 minutes
Baking Time: 8 to 10 minutes

INGREDIENTS

1-1/2	CUPS BUTTER *OR* MARGARINE, SOFTENED
1	CUP GRANULATED SUGAR
1	TABLESPOON GRATED LEMON PEEL
1	TEASPOON GROUND GINGER
1/8	TEASPOON GROUND CLOVES
1	EGG
1	TEASPOON LEMON JUICE
3-1/2	CUPS ALL-PURPOSE FLOUR
	SLIVERED CRYSTALLIZED GINGER (OPTIONAL)
	CANDIED LEMON PEEL (OPTIONAL)

Bits of crystallized ginger and candied lemon peel top these cookies and give a hint of their flavor.

Orange Marmalade Wreaths

Preparation Time: 30 minutes
Baking Time: 7 to 9 minutes

INGREDIENTS

COOKIES

- 1 CUP BUTTER *OR* MARGARINE, SOFTENED
- 3/4 CUP SIFTED POWDERED SUGAR
- 2 TEASPOONS GRATED ORANGE PEEL
- 2 CUPS ALL-PURPOSE FLOUR

FILLING

- 1 3-OUNCE PACKAGE CREAM CHEESE, SOFTENED
- 2 TABLESPOONS ORANGE MARMALADE

DRIZZLE (OPTIONAL)

- 1/4 CUP SEMISWEET CHOCOLATE PIECES
- 1/2 TEASPOON SHORTENING

Dress up these wreaths by drizzling melted chocolate over them. For the winter holidays, press snipped pieces of red and green maraschino cherries into the drizzled chocolate while it's still warm.

■ For cookies, in a large mixing bowl beat the butter or margarine with an electric mixer on medium to high speed for 30 seconds. Add the powdered sugar and orange peel; beat till combined. Beat in as much of the flour as you can with the mixer. Stir in any remaining flour with a wooden spoon. Do not chill the dough.

■ Pack dough into a cookie press fitted with a wreath plate. Force dough through the cookie press in wreath shapes 1 inch apart onto ungreased cookie sheets.

■ Bake in a preheated 375° oven for 7 to 9 minutes, or till edges are firm but not brown. Remove cookies from pans and cool on a rack.

■ For filling, in a small mixing bowl stir together the cream cheese and orange marmalade. Spread 1 teaspoon of the cream cheese-marmalade mixture over the flat side of half of the cookies; top with remaining cookies, flat sides down.

■ If desired, for drizzle, in a small, heavy saucepan melt chocolate pieces and shortening over low heat. Drizzle over cookies.

Makes about 20 cookies

Per cookie: 159 calories, 2 g protein, 14 g carbohydrate, 11 g total fat (7 g saturated), 25 mg cholesterol, 121 mg sodium, 23 mg potassium

STEPS AT A GLANCE	Page
MAKING COOKIE DOUGH	8
MAKING PRESSED COOKIES	96
DRIZZLING ICING OR CHOCOLATE	11

Festive cookie wreaths, filled with rich cream cheese and orange marmalade and drizzled with chocolate, will brighten any cookie assortment.

Specialty Cookies

Steps for Making Madeleines

BASIC TOOLS FOR MAKING MADELEINES

You'll need bowls and a rubber spatula for mixing the batter, a pastry brush and a madeleine pan for baking, and a rack and mesh sieve for finishing the cookies.

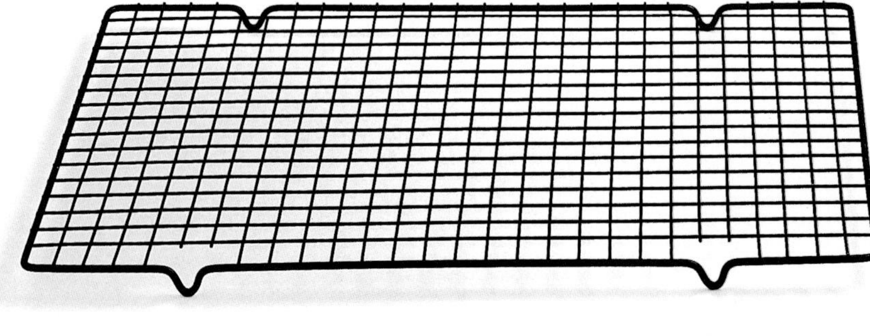

MIXING BOWLS AND FINE-MESHED SIEVE

MADELEINE PAN

RUBBER SPATULA

KNIFE

PASTRY BRUSH

DELICATE MADELEINES, like the other cookies in this chapter, aren't easily categorized. These French tea cookies resemble tiny sponge cakes, yet they are not baked in a cake pan. Instead they are formed in small shell-shaped molds that each produce a single portion. But no matter what you call them, the result is an ethereal dessert, especially when eaten soon after they cool.

Traditional madeleine pans are made of tinned steel and are available in kitchenware stores or from catalogs that specialize in cooking equipment. A pan for standard-size madeleines like those shown on the next page typically has 12 molds, each 3 inches long from the top of the shell to its base. Before baking, the molds must be brushed with melted butter or margarine so the fragile cookies will release easily after baking.

Madeleines will be especially light, airy, and moist if you keep two simple hints in mind when you prepare them. First, beat the sugar and eggs thoroughly (at least 5 minutes or more) until the mixture makes a thick, satiny ribbon on the surface of the batter when the beaters are lifted. Second, blend the batter with care so it doesn't deflate, especially when folding in the dry ingredients.

SPICED MADELEINES

Preparation Time: 30 minutes
Baking Time: 10 to 12 minutes

INGREDIENTS

4	EGGS
1	TEASPOON VANILLA
2/3	CUP GRANULATED SUGAR
1-1/3	CUPS ALL-PURPOSE FLOUR
1	TEASPOON GROUND CINNAMON
1/2	TEASPOON BAKING POWDER
1/4	TEASPOON GROUND NUTMEG
1/2	CUP MARGARINE *OR* BUTTER, MELTED AND COOLED
	POWDERED SUGAR

■ In a large mixing bowl beat eggs and vanilla with an electric mixer on high speed for 5 minutes. Gradually beat in the sugar. Beat for 5 to 7 minutes, or till thick and satiny.

■ In a medium mixing bowl sift together the flour, cinnamon, baking powder, and nutmeg. Sift one fourth of the flour mixture over egg mixture; gently fold in. Fold in remaining flour by fourths. Fold in the ½ cup butter or margarine. Spoon batter into greased madeleine molds, filling each one three-fourths full.

■ Bake in a preheated 375° oven for 10 to 12 minutes, or till edges are golden and tops spring back. Cool in molds on a rack for 1 minute.

■ Transfer cookies to a rack and cool. Sift powdered sugar over tops. Store in freezer.

Makes about 30 madeleines

Per madeleine: 75 calories, 1 g protein, 9 g carbohydrate, 4 g total fat (2 g saturated), 37 mg cholesterol, 45 mg sodium, 16 mg potassium

the bristles of a pastry brush will reach every crevice of the mold

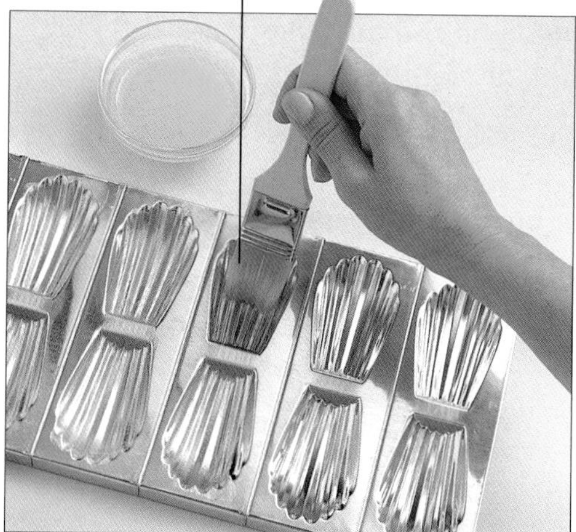

STEP 1 GREASING MOLDS

With a pastry brush, completely coat each madeleine mold with melted butter or margarine, making sure that each groove is coated so the finished cookies won't stick to the pan. Or spray with nonstick spray coating.

the two mixtures will blend more easily if only a portion of the dry ingredients is added at a time

STEP 2 FOLDING FLOUR INTO EGGS

Sift one fourth of the flour mixture over the egg mixture. Gently fold by cutting down through the center with the edge of a rubber spatula, coming across the bottom of the bowl, then lifting up along the side of the bowl in one smooth motion.

you can also invert the mold over the wire rack to remove the cookies, but they may be damaged as they fall out

STEP 3 REMOVING MADELEINES

After the cookies have finished baking, let them cool in the pan for 1 minute. Loosen each cookie with a knife or skewer, then lift it out of the pan and place on a wire rack.

you can also use a powdered-sugar canister to apply the topping

STEP 4 SIFTING POWDERED SUGAR

Place all the madeleines ridged-side up on the rack. Spoon some powdered sugar into a fine-meshed sieve or perforated canister and tap it to lightly dust the tops of the cookies.

Part sponge cake, part cookie, sugar-dusted madeleines are a classic French confection. The recipe for Spiced Madeleines appears on the opposite page.

Ladyfingers

STEPS AT A GLANCE	Page
LINING COOKIE SHEET	18
MAKING LADYFINGERS	110

Preparation Time: 45 minutes
Baking Time: 8 to 10 minutes

INGREDIENTS

- 4 EGG WHITES
- 1/2 CUP SIFTED POWDERED SUGAR
- 4 EGG YOLKS
- 1 TEASPOON VANILLA
- 3/4 CUP SIFTED CAKE FLOUR
- 4 TEASPOONS POWDERED SUGAR

These dainty and versatile sponge cakes can be made into sandwiches with jam or preserves, used to line a dessert mold, or simply served with fresh fruit and a cup of tea.

■ In a large mixing bowl let the egg whites stand at room temperature for 30 minutes. Line a cookie sheet with parchment paper or brown kraft paper. Set aside. In a large mixing bowl beat egg whites with an electric mixer on high speed till soft peaks form (tips curl). Gradually add ¼ cup of the powdered sugar, beating till stiff peaks form (tips stand straight).

■ In a small mixing bowl beat the egg yolks on medium speed for 1 minute. Gradually add the remaining one fourth cup powdered sugar, beating on high speed till thick and lemon colored, 4 to 5 minutes. Stir in vanilla. By hand, fold egg yolk mixture into egg whites. Gradually fold in cake flour about one fourth at a time. Spoon batter into a pastry bag fitted with a large round tip (about ½ inch in diameter). Pipe 3½ x ¾-inch strips of batter 1 inch apart on the prepared cookie sheet. (Or, spoon batter into lightly greased ladyfinger molds till batter is even with top of pan.) Sift 4 teaspoons powdered sugar over cookies.

■ Bake in a preheated 350° oven for 8 to 10 minutes, or till lightly browned. Transfer cookies on paper or in ladyfinger molds to a rack; cool about 10 minutes. Remove ladyfingers from the paper or molds, then cool completely on the rack. Store in the freezer.

Makes about 36 ladyfingers

Per ladyfinger: 24 calories, 1 g protein, 4 g carbohydrate, 1 g total fat (0 g saturated), 24 mg cholesterol, 7 mg sodium, 10 mg potassium

STEPS FOR MAKING LADYFINGERS

STEP 1 PIPING COOKIES

Line cookie sheets with parchment paper or brown kraft paper. Spoon the batter into a pastry bag fitted with a ½-inch round tip. Lay the bag almost parallel with the cookie sheet and, using even pressure, pipe out 3½x¾-inch strips of dough.

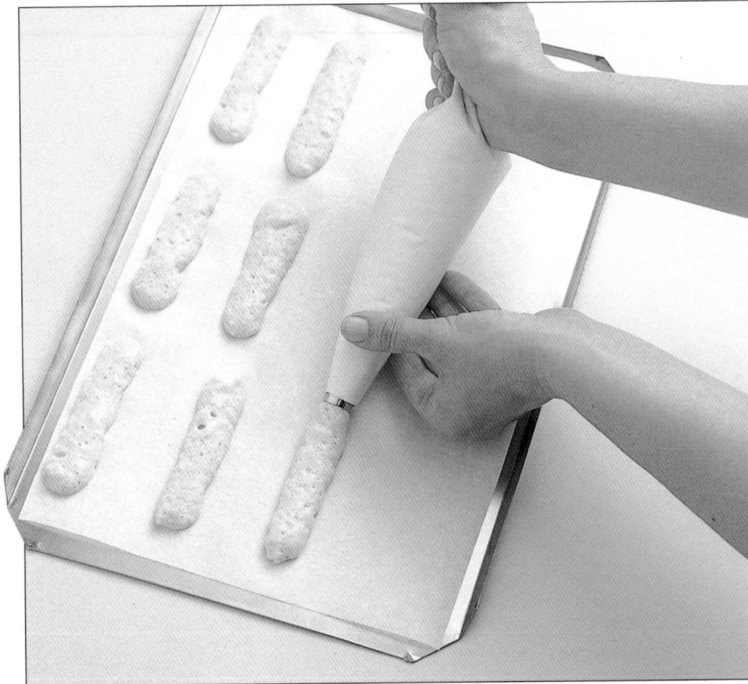

STEP 2 SIFTING SUGAR

Sprinkle the ladyfingers with powdered sugar from a powdered sugar canister or a fine-meshed sieve. Then bake.

A coating of powdered sugar melts into the fragrant dough as these ladyfingers bake, infusing them with a wonderful depth of flavor. Dust with sugar again before serving.

Biscotti are baked twice to slowly dry them into crunchy rusks that Italians enjoy dipped in coffee or Vin Santo, a sweet dessert wine.

Biscotti

Preparation Time: 35 minutes
Baking Time: 40 to 43 minutes

INGREDIENTS

1	CUP GRANULATED SUGAR
1	TEASPOON BAKING SODA
1/4	TEASPOON SALT
3	EGGS
1	TEASPOON VANILLA
1/2	TEASPOON ALMOND EXTRACT
2-3/4	CUPS ALL-PURPOSE FLOUR
1	CUP FINELY CHOPPED SLIVERED ALMONDS, WALNUTS, PECANS, PINE NUTS, MACADAMIA NUTS, *OR* HAZELNUTS
1	BEATEN EGG
1	TEASPOON WATER

Biscotti are a traditional Italian treat often served with strong, hot coffee. The small, crisp slices are made for dunking. For a spiced version, omit the almond extract and stir in ½ teaspoon ground cinnamon, ¼ teaspoon ground cloves, and ¼ teaspoon ground nutmeg.

■ In a large mixing bowl stir together the sugar, baking soda, and salt. Stir in 3 eggs, vanilla, and almond extract. Stir in the flour and chopped nuts.

■ On a well-floured surface, knead dough 8 to 10 times. Divide in half. On a lightly floured surface shape each half into a log about 9 inches long. Place logs about 4 inches apart on a lightly greased cookie sheet. Pat each log into a flattened loaf about 10 inches long and 2¼ inches wide. Stir together the egg and water; brush over loaves.

■ Bake in a preheated 325° oven for 30 minutes. Cool on a rack. Cut each loaf diagonally into ½-inch-thick slices. Place slices, cut-sides down, on ungreased cookie sheets. Bake in the 325° oven for 5 minutes. Turn slices over and bake for 5 to 8 minutes more, or till dry and crisp. Remove cookies from pan and cool on a rack.

Makes about 38 biscotti

Per cookie: 75 calories, 2 g protein, 12 g carbohydrate, 2 g total fat (0 g saturated), 22 mg cholesterol, 54 mg sodium, 37 mg potassium

STEPS AT A GLANCE	Page
MAKING BISCOTTI	113

STEPS FOR MAKING BISCOTTI

STEP 1 CUTTING COOKIES

Bake the loaves for 30 minutes, then cool. Place a loaf on a cutting board and slice diagonally into ½-inch-thick slices with a sharp, thin-bladed or serrated knife. Repeat with the other loaf.

STEP 2 SECOND BAKING

Place the slices cut-side down on ungreased baking sheets. Bake for 5 minutes, then turn them over and bake until the cookies are dry and crisp, another 5 to 8 minutes. Cool them on a wire rack.

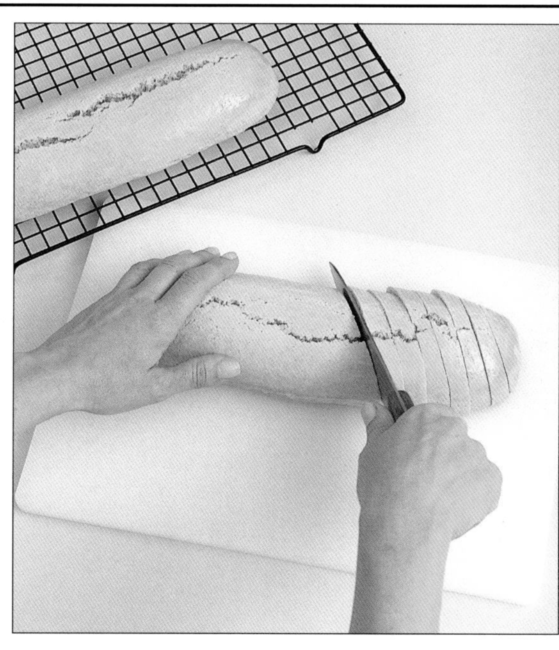

Chocolate-dipped Mushrooms

STEPS AT A GLANCE	Page
MAKING MERINGUE	11
LINING COOKIE SHEET	18
MAKING MUSHROOMS	114

Preparation Time: 45 minutes
Baking Time: 20 to 25 minutes
Drying Time: 30 minutes

INGREDIENTS

3	EGG WHITES
1/2	TEASPOON VANILLA
1/4	TEASPOON CREAM OF TARTAR
3/4	CUP GRANULATED SUGAR
4	OUNCES SEMISWEET CHOCOLATE
2	TABLESPOONS SIFTED POWDERED SUGAR
2	TEASPOONS UNSWEETENED COCOA POWDER

If you want spotted mushrooms, use a toothpick or a small, new paintbrush to "paint" spots of melted chocolate on the mushroom caps. Try to make these cookies on a cool, dry day, as humidity or rain tends to make meringue soft or cause it to bead.

■ In a medium mixing bowl let egg whites stand at room temperature for 30 minutes. Meanwhile, line 2 cookie sheets with parchment paper or brown kraft paper. Set aside.

■ Add the vanilla and cream of tartar to egg whites. Beat with an electric mixer on medium speed till soft peaks form (tips curl). Gradually add sugar, 1 tablespoon at a time, beating on high speed till very stiff peaks form (tips stand straight) and sugar is almost dissolved. Spoon egg white mixture into a decorating bag fitted with a large round tip (½-inch opening). Pipe about two thirds of the meringue mixture into 1½-inch-diameter mounds about 1 inch apart onto prepared cookie sheets. With remaining meringue, pipe 1-inch-tall bases about ½ inch apart on cookie sheets. (To get an even number of caps and stems, pipe one cap, then one stem, until all meringue is used.)

■ Bake in a preheated 300° oven for 20 to 25 minutes, or till cookies just begin to brown. Turn off oven. Let cookies dry in oven with the door closed for 30 minutes. Remove cookies from pans and cool on a rack.

■ In a small, heavy saucepan heat chocolate over low heat till melted. Spread a scant ½ teaspoon of the melted chocolate on the underside of each mushroom cap. Attach stems by inserting top ends in center of melted chocolate mixture, pressing gently into cookie. Let mushrooms dry upside down on racks until chocolate is set.

■ To serve, combine powdered sugar and cocoa powder. Sift over the tops of mushrooms.

Makes about 55 cookies

Per cookie: 22 calories, 0 g protein, 4 g carbohydrate, 1 g total fat (0 g saturated), 0 mg cholesterol, 3 mg sodium, 12 mg potassium

STEPS FOR MAKING MUSHROOMS

STEP 1 Piping Parts

Gently squeeze out caps and stems onto a paper-lined cookie sheet using a pastry bag filled with the egg white–sugar mixture. To create nicely rounded caps, hold the piping tip close to the cookie sheet.

STEP 2 Adding Stems

Spread ½ teaspoon of melted chocolate on the underside of each meringue cap. Insert the pointed end of a stem into each cap, pressing slightly to secure. Dry upside down on a rack until the chocolate sets.

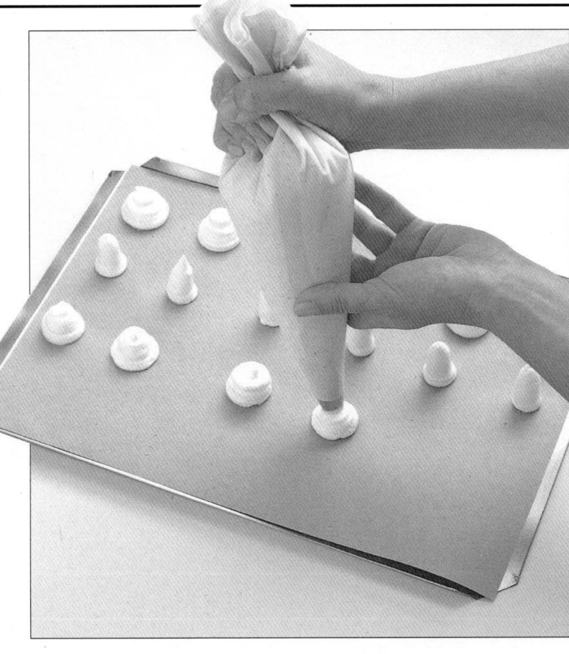

Meringue mushrooms with chocolate "gills" are a charming treat on their own, and they also are a classic decoration for a *Bûche de Noël,* or Christmas Log.

A triangle of tangy sour-cream dough enfolds a filling of apricot preserves and chopped white baking bar (white chocolate).

White Chocolate–Apricot Rugelach

Preparation Time: 45 minutes
Baking Time: 20 to 25 minutes

INGREDIENTS

1-3/4	CUPS ALL-PURPOSE FLOUR
3/4	CUP COLD BUTTER *OR* MARGARINE
1/2	CUP DAIRY SOUR CREAM
1	TEASPOON VANILLA
1/3	CUP APRICOT *OR* RASPBERRY PRESERVES, *OR* ORANGE MARMALADE
3	OUNCES WHITE BAKING BAR, FINELY CHOPPED (1/2 CUP)
2	TABLESPOONS GRANULATED SUGAR
1	TEASPOON GROUND CINNAMON (OPTIONAL)

These pastrylike goodies are a treat for breakfast or with tea as well as after dinner. Choose your favorite flavor of preserves or marmalade for the filling.

■ Place flour in a mixing bowl. With a pastry blender or 2 knives, cut in butter or margarine till mixture resembles small peas. Stir in the sour cream and vanilla just till dough holds together. On a lightly floured surface, knead dough about 10 times. Divide dough in thirds. Wrap in plastic wrap.

■ On a lightly floured surface, roll one third of the dough into a 10-inch circle. Spread dough with a scant 2 tablespoons of the preserves or marmalade. Sprinkle with one third of the chopped white baking bar. Cut dough into 12 wedges. Starting at curved edge, roll up each wedge jelly-roll style. Place, point-side down, 2 inches apart on an ungreased cookie sheet. Repeat with remaining dough, preserves or marmalade, and white baking bar.

■ In a small mixing bowl stir together the sugar and, if desired, cinnamon; sprinkle over each cookie.

■ Bake in a preheated 375° oven for 20 to 25 minutes, or till light golden brown. Remove cookies from pans and cool on a rack. Store in a tightly covered container.

Makes about 36 cookies

Per cookie: 85 calories, 1 g protein, 9 g carbohydrate, 5 g total fat (3 g saturated), 12 mg cholesterol, 49 mg sodium, 22 mg potassium

STEPS AT A GLANCE	Page
CUTTING IN BUTTER OR MARGARINE	34
MAKING RUGELACH	117

STEPS FOR MAKING RUGELACH

STEP 1 CUTTING DOUGH
Roll out one third of the dough into a 10-inch circle on a lightly floured surface and cover with fillings. With a plain or fluted pastry cutter or small chef's knife divide the dough into 12 equal wedges.

STEP 2 SHAPING COOKIE
Starting at the curved edge of one of the wedges, roll it toward the point, enclosing the filling. Arrange point-side down on an ungreased cookie sheet. Repeat with remaining wedges. Leave 2 inches between each rolled cookie.

GLOSSARY

The following glossary provides information on selecting, purchasing, and storing ingredients used in this book. Groups of ingredients are arranged clockwise from the upper left and are described in the text accordingly.

BANANAS

BUTTER BRICKLE PIECES

CHOCOLATE

COCONUT

COFFEE

BANANAS Tropical bananas are usually yellow-skinned, with creamy, sweet flesh, although some varieties have red skin and pink flesh. Use slightly overripe bananas for baking. Green or unripe bananas will ripen in a few days at room temperature. Store ripe bananas in the refrigerator for several days.

BUTTER BRICKLE PIECES Brickle is another name for brittle, that rich, golden-brown, buttery hard candy. Add packaged brickle pieces to cookie doughs and batters as directed in the recipe. Available in the baking section of most supermarkets, these are sometimes called "toffee bits."

CHOCOLATE The following chocolate types are commonly used in baking. *Sweet chocolate* contains at least 15 percent pure chocolate, extra cocoa butter, and sugar. *Unsweetened chocolate* is pure chocolate with no sugar or flavoring, while *cocoa powder* is pure chocolate with very little cocoa butter. Because it lacks pure chocolate, *white baking bar* (white chocolate) can't be considered a true chocolate product, although it does contain cocoa butter. *Semisweet chocolate pieces* or *chips* are interchangeable with coarsely chopped *semisweet chocolate*. Store well wrapped in a cool, dry place for up to 4 months.

COCONUT The dried meat of the coconut palm adds an exotic note to cookies. It is widely available in a number of forms, including shredded and flaked, either sweetened or unsweetened. It will keep for months if stored airtight.

COFFEE Instant coffee crystals and instant espresso powder are preferred for baking because of their intense flavor and because they blend easily into batters and doughs. They will keep indefinitely if stored airtight.

COOKING FATS Butter, margarine, and vegetable shortening make cookies tender. Butter and margarine are interchangeable in almost all cookie recipes. However, margarine made from 100 percent corn oil will make a very soft cookie dough that may require a longer chilling time to prevent the dough from spreading too much during baking. Use only regular stick margarine, not diet, whipped, or liquid forms. Shortening is a vegetable oil–based fat manufactured to stay solid at room temperature. Butter and margarine will keep for 1 month, well wrapped in the refrigerator, or up to 6 months in the freezer. Store shortening at room temperature for up to 1 year.

CREAM CHEESE Made from a mixture of cow's cream and milk, cream cheese is appreciated for its smooth, spreadable consistency and mild, slightly tangy flavor. Available in bricks and in bulk. Refrigerate and use within a week.

DRIED FRUIT Drying intensifies the natural flavor of fruit and concentrates its sweetness. Dried fruit, including dates, apricots, and figs, is a favorite addition to cookies. Unopened packages of dried fruit will stay wholesome almost indefinitely. Once opened, transfer to a plastic bag and store in the refrigerator.

EGGS Cookies acquire flavor, tenderness, richness, and structure from eggs, although not every cookie recipe uses eggs. Shell color — brown or white — is purely superficial; there is no difference in quality. Refrigerate in the carton for up to 5 weeks.

FLOUR Wheat flour gives cookies their structure. All-purpose flour has a medium protein content that makes it suitable for most baking uses, while cake flour is lower in protein for a fine-textured crumb. Whole-wheat flour is coarsely milled from the entire wheat kernel. Store white flour in an airtight container for 10 to 15 months; store whole-grain for up to 5 months. Or, refrigerate or freeze for longer storage.

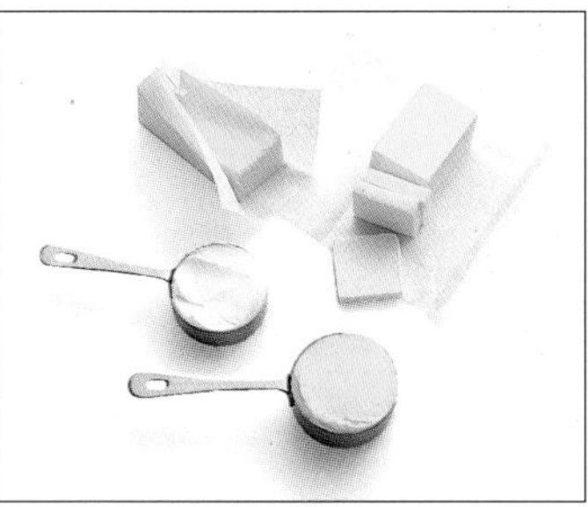

COOKING FATS

CREAM CHEESE

DRIED FRUIT

EGGS

FLOUR

GINGER

JELLIES AND PRESERVES

LEAVENERS

NUTS

PUMPKIN

GINGER The rhizome, or underground stem, of a semitropical plant, ginger is marketed fresh, dried and ground into a powder, and as crystallized or "candied" bits preserved in a syrup and coated in sugar. Select fresh gingerroots that are firm, not shriveled. Wrap in a paper towel and refrigerate for 2 to 3 weeks. Store ground and crystallized ginger for up to 6 months.

JELLIES AND PRESERVES Whether sandwiched between two cookie rounds, dropped in the middle of a chewy morsel, or swirled through rich bar cookie batter, jellies and preserves add jewellike color and fruity flavor to cookies of all kinds. Be sure to use the best-quality spreads you can find, with true fruit flavor that isn't masked by too much sugar.

LEAVENERS Chemical leaveners give cookies a boost so they rise as they bake. *Baking powder* reacts with liquid and/or heat to produce bubbles of carbon dioxide that cause batters and doughs to expand. When exposed to moisture and an acidic ingredient like buttermilk, yogurt, chocolate, or lemon juice, *baking soda* also releases carbon dioxide gas. *Cream of tartar* is commonly mixed with commercial baking soda and, by itself, is added to beaten egg whites as a stabilizer. Replace baking powder every 3 months.

NUTS Almonds, hazelnuts, macadamias, peanuts, pecans, pine nuts, pistachios, and walnuts add richness, texture, and flavor to cookie doughs and fillings. You'll find them in supermarkets packaged and in bulk in a number of forms, shelled and unshelled. Store, tightly covered, in the refrigerator or freezer.

PUMPKIN During the cool months, this winter squash finds its way into breads, cakes, pies, and cookies of all kinds, enhanced by spices like cinnamon, nutmeg, ginger, cloves, and allspice. Convenient canned pumpkin purée is available all year.

RAISINS These dried grapes are well-loved cookie additions. Every market sells them in boxes, packages, and in bulk. Dark seedless raisins have deep color and flavor, while golden seedless are pale and tangy. Dark and golden raisins are interchangeable in recipes, but *raisins* in an ingredients list usually means the former. Store unopened packages in a dry place; once opened, seal and refrigerate or freeze.

ROLLED OATS When oats are steamed, then flattened by steel rollers into flakes, they are sold as rolled oats or old-fashioned oats. Quick-cooking oats and rolled oats can be used interchangeably. They add bulk and flavor to cookies. Store airtight for up to 6 months or freeze for up to 1 year.

SPICES For centuries, spices like cinnamon, cloves, allspice, nutmeg, and ginger have added their distinctive character to baked goods. In the market, all spices are available dried. Spices lose flavor after about 6 months if ground and after 2 years if whole. Store in a cool, dark, dry place.

SUGARS These sweeteners add flavor and color to cookie doughs and batters, fillings, and frostings: *Dark brown sugar* is a mixture of granulated sugar and molasses that adds rich, deep flavor. *Light brown sugar* has less molasses flavor than dark brown sugar. *Powdered sugar,* also called *confectioners' sugar,* is ground and mixed with a small amount of cornstarch to prevent caking. Typically, it is used for frostings and coatings. *Granulated sugar* is available in fine white crystals (most common) and superfine (for frostings and meringues). Store sugars indefinitely in airtight containers.

SWEETENERS, LIQUID Liquid sweeteners add their own character to cookies. Made by bees from floral nectar, *honey* is sweet and sticky and imparts rich flavor and perfume to batters, doughs, and fillings. *Molasses* is a by-product of sugar-cane refining. *Light molasses* is sweet and mild; *dark molasses* is less sweet and more full-bodied. They are interchangeable in recipes. Unopened bottles of syrup last up to a year in a cool spot; after opening, store as directed on the label. Syrup and honey will pour off more freely from a measuring spoon or cup if either is first lightly oiled.

RAISINS

ROLLED OATS

SPICES

SUGARS

SWEETENERS, LIQUID

INDEX

Recipes

Almond cookies
- almond crisps 82–83
- almond half-moons 98–99
- amaretti 18–19
- glazed almond strips 102–103
- Linzer sandwich rings 56–57

Amaretti 18–19
Anise cookies
- anise butterflies 104
- koulourakia 93

Apricot cookies
- apricot macaroon bars 46
- white chocolate–apricot rugelach 116–117

Biscotti 112–113
Blonde brownies 43
Bonbons, peanut butter 90
Brownies
- blonde brownies 43
- chocolate-raspberry brownies 38–39
- mocha brownies 42

Butterflies, anise 104
Carrot-raisin drops 27
Checkerboards, chocolate & vanilla 70–71
Cheesecake dreams, orange 36–37
Cherry-chocolate parson's hats 63
Chocolate cookies
- blonde brownies 43
- chocolate butter spritz 100–101
- chocolate-cherry parson's hats 63
- chocolate-coconut meringue bars 48
- chocolate-dipped mushrooms 114–115
- chocolate-drizzled praline cookies 16–17
- chocolate-kahlúa truffle cookies 88
- chocolate-peppermint slices 76
- chocolate-pistachio sandwich cookies 72–73
- chocolate-raspberry brownies 38–39
- chocolate & vanilla checkerboards 70–71
- espresso meringue kisses 25
- hazelnut toffee bars 41
- mocha brownies 42
- mocha tea cookies 75
- peanut butter bonbons 90
- Rocky Road sandwich cookies 78
- triple-chocolate cookies 24

Cinnamon snails 91
Coconut cookies
- apricot macaroon bars 46
- chocolate-coconut meringue bars 48
- coconut-macadamia cookies 28
- coconut-orange wafers 77

Coffee cookies
- coffee-pecan triangles 45
- espresso meringue kisses 25
- mocha brownies 42
- mocha tea cookies 75

Date triangles, sour cream– 44
Espresso meringue kisses 25
Fig-orange drops 26
Florentines, pecan 89
Frosted lime wafers 30
Fruity foldovers 66
Gingerbread dough & icing 53
Ginger cookies
- lemon-ginger tea cookies 105
- molasses & ginger stars 64

Glazed almond strips 102–103
Half-moons, almond 98–99
Hazelnut toffee bars 41
Holiday cookies 62
Honey snowflakes 58–59
Ice cream sandwiches 22–23
Koulourakia 93
Ladyfingers 110–111
Lemon cookies
- lemon-ginger tea cookies 105
- lemon-pistachio pretzels 92
- meringue-topped lemon thins 65

Lime wafers, frosted 30
Linzer sandwich rings 56–57
Macadamia-coconut cookies 28
Madeleines, spiced 108
Meringue-topped lemon thins 65
Mocha brownies 42
Mocha tea cookies 75
Molasses & ginger stars 64
Mushrooms, chocolate-dipped 114–115
Orange cookies
- coconut-orange wafers 77
- orange cheesecake dreams 36–37
- orange-fig drops 26
- orange marmalade wreaths 106
- raspberry-orange strips 86–87

Parson's hats, chocolate-cherry 63
Peanut butter cookies
- peanut butter bonbons 90
- peanut butter brickle drops 29

Pecan cookies
- chocolate-drizzled praline cookies 16–17
- coffee-pecan triangles 45
- pecan florentines 89

Peppermint-chocolate slices 76
Pinwheels, raspberry 60–61
Pistachio cookies
- chocolate-pistachio sandwich cookies 72–73
- lemon-pistachio pretzels 92

Praline cookies, chocolate-drizzled 16–17
Pretzels, lemon-pistachio 92
Pumpkin spice bars 47
Raisin-carrot drops 27
Raspberry cookies
- chocolate-raspberry brownies 38–39
- Linzer sandwich rings 56–57
- raspberry-orange strips 86–87
- raspberry pinwheels 60–61

Rocky Road sandwich cookies 78
Rugelach, white chocolate–apricot 116–117
Rum & spice cookies 74
Sesame fork cookies 94
Shortbread 84–85
Snails, cinnamon 91
Snowflakes, honey 58–59
Sour cream–date triangles 44
Spiced madeleines 108
Stars, molasses & ginger 64
Trail mix cookies 20–21
Triple-chocolate cookies 24
Truffle cookies, chocolate-kahlúa 88
White chocolate–apricot rugelach 116–117
Wreaths, orange marmalade 106

Step by Steps

Almond strips, making 102
Bar cookies, making 32–33
Bar cookies with a crust, making 34–35
Biscotti, making 113
Checkerboard cookies, making 70
Chocolate, piping 17
Cookie dough, making 8–9
Cookies
- shaping and molding 80–81
- storing 12

Crumb topping, making 37
Cutout cookies, making 50–51
Drop cookies, making 14–15
Fruit, preparing 20
Gingerbread cottage, making 52–55
Half-moons, shaping 98
Ladyfingers, making 110
Madeleines, making 108–109
Melted topping, making 41
Meringue, making 10–11
Mushrooms, making 114
Nuts, grinding 18
Pans, preparing 18
Pinwheels, making 60
Pirouettes, shaping 82
Pressed cookies, making 96–97
Rugelach, making 117
Sandwich cookies, making 73
"Sandwiches," making 22
Sandwich rings, making 56
Shortbread, shaping 85
Sliced cookies, making 68–69
Snowflakes, decorating 59
Spritz cookies, decorating 101
Strips, making 86
Swirled topping, making 38
Toppings, making 10–11
Tulip cups, shaping 82

Using the Nutrition Analysis

Keep track of your daily nutrition needs by using the information we provide at the end of each recipe. We've analyzed the nutritional content of each recipe serving for you. When a recipe gives an ingredient substitution, we used the first choice in the analysis. If it makes a range of servings (such as 4 to 6), we used the smaller number. Ingredients listed as optional weren't included in the calculations.